EUCHARIST: A GUIDE FOR THE PERPLEXED

T&T Clark Guides for the Perplexed

T&T Clark's Guides for the Perplexed are clear, concise and accessible introductions to thinkers, writers and subjects that students and readers can find especially challenging. Concentrating specifically on what it is that makes the subject difficult to grasp, these books explain and explore key themes and ideas, guiding the reader towards a thorough understanding of demanding material.

Guides for the Perplexed available from T&T Clark:

De Lubac: A Guide for the Perplexed, David Grumett
Christian Bioethics: A Guide for the Perplexed, Agneta Sutton
Calvin: A Guide for the Perplexed, Paul Helm
Tillich: A Guide for the Perplexed, Andrew O'Neill
The Trinity: A Guide for the Perplexed, Paul M. Collins
Christology: A Guide for the Perplexed, Alan Spence
Wesley: A Guide for the Perplexed, Jason E. Vickers
Pannenberg: A Guide for the Perplexed, Timothy Bradshaw
Balthasar: A Guide for the Perplexed, Rodney Howsare
Theological Anthropology: A Guide for the Perplexed, Marc Cortez
Bonhoeffer: A Guide for the Perplexed, Joel Lawrence
Benedict XVI: A Guide for the Perplexed, Tracey Rowland

Forthcoming titles:

Church: A Guide for the Perplexed, Matt Jenson and David Wilhite
Interfaith Relations: A Guide for the Perplexed, Jeffrey Bailey

EUCHARIST: A GUIDE FOR THE PERPLEXED

RALPH N. McMICHAEL

t&t clark

Published by T&T Clark International
A Continuum Imprint
The Tower Building   80 Maiden Lane
11 York Road   Suite 704
London SE1 7NX   New York NY 10038

www.continuumbooks.com

British Library Cataloguing-in-Publication Data
A catalogue record for this book is available from the British Library

ISBN-13:   978-0-567-03228-7 (Hardback)
           978-0-567-03229-4 (Paperback)

Typeset by Newgen Imaging Systems Pvt Ltd, Chennai, India
Printed and bound in Great Britain by the MPG Books Group

CONTENTS

ACKNOWLEDGMENTS

A book is the product of many influences, both explicit and implicit ones. Certainly, an author takes up the task of writing having been shaped by many people and an array of ideas. Appropriately, this is the case for me and for a book on the Eucharist, the sacrament of communion. My sharing in the Eucharistic life began with my parents: Ralph and Marinell. My study of this life was initiated and inspired by Louis Weil. Any growth and maturity in the life of the Eucharist was fostered by the numerous students and parishioners where I have taught and prayed, serving as theologian and as priest. Special thanks are due to Pamela Dolan and Marshall Crossnoe, who read the manuscript and offered their editing skills, support, and friendship. Most of all, I am grateful to those persons with whom I share a loving and faithful communion of life: Nelson, Anne Marie, Breck, and wonderfully with Jan.

INTRODUCTION

What is the Eucharist? At first, this might seem a straightforward question. However, any canvassing of a group of Christians, especially if they are members of different denominations, would reveal an array of answers that might not be recognized as answers to the same question. In fact, the question itself implies one such direction for its answer by the presence of the term Eucharist. For the subject of this study has, and does go by, many names, the Eucharist being one of them. Other names or terms for this subject include Lord's Supper, the Mass, Holy Communion, and the Divine Liturgy. Eucharist itself has referred to a complete rite or ritual event as well as to a specific part or object within this event. Each of these names has a history of theological exposition, controversy, and ecclesial identity. Furthermore, this history of multiple ecclesial and theological developments is viewed today from a plurality of liturgical rites existing not only within an array of churches but within an array of cultures and of languages. Eucharistic celebration and understanding can also be shaped by our heightened postmodern awareness of difference and otherness. Any attempt to resolve this plurality by the identification and enforcement of a singular and universal Eucharistic celebration and theology would prove futile. Despite various ecumenical efforts and achievements, we still view a Eucharistic landscape that is diverse, and in some ways fragmented.

The reader might ask at this point, so what? Is a uniform and universal Eucharistic rite and understanding desirable? Would the task of identifying a normative Eucharist, with an accompanying theology, be appropriate in light of our acknowledgement that we live in a multichurch, multicultural, multilingual, and even multireligious world? This depends on our reference(s) for appropriateness. What constitutes an appropriate Eucharistic celebration and understanding? Are these appropriate questions for a reflection on the Eucharist? And, what is the purpose and goal of our questioning? What is the

1

question that lies behind all of our questioning, the question, whether we realize it or not, that generates the questions we ask and maintains the silence of the questions we do not ask?

Let us return to our starting question—What is the Eucharist? This is a question of identity, a quest for recognition that would be guided by the perception of a normative structure and enactment. Presumably, one could reach a point in this quest where a structure of enactment, or ritual, could be identified as a Eucharist or not. We could have a basis for declaring what is, and what is not, a Eucharist. Our criteria for assessment would emphasize what constitutes the Eucharist and what abides as its normative enactment. ("Celebration" of the Eucharist is a term that bears an attributive meaning; it is not neutral, but it will serve as our regular reference to the act of Eucharist.) The what-question leads to the particulars of what makes a Eucharist qua Eucharist and to its recognizable performance. That is, the what-question addressed to the Eucharist implies the how-question. How is the Eucharist done? The Eucharist is an event, a corporate action, and as such, it allows for evaluation of its performance.

The primary generative question is not what or how, as critical as these questions are, but why. Why the Eucharist? This question lies behind all of our questioning regarding the Eucharist. It is a question that must be remembered as we explore all other questions so that we do not forget what kinds of understandings, performances, or life the Eucharist allows and makes possible. Fidelity to the why-question exists as the Eucharistic gaze. This gaze has two visional directions: The presence of the Triune God offering us the sacrificial invitation to share in the Son's life of communion; and, the way this transformative gift of communion exists for the life of the world. These two directions or horizons of the Eucharistic gaze provide the appropriate guide for all the myriad of questions, controversies, performances, and understandings that have arisen about the Eucharist. The twofold horizon of the Eucharistic gaze—God's invitation to communion and for the life of the world—is our guide for all types of Eucharistic perplexity.

The Eucharistic gaze allows for the recognition of the unexpected, the familiar receptivity of the strange gift, and for the life that beckons beyond the horizon of our own portraiture. To gaze at something or someone involves a level of fascination beyond the usual noticing or practiced awareness. A gaze is a fixed attention that may not be conscious or premeditated. We gaze because we are drawn toward an object or toward a subject that somehow requires a space and a time from us so that an unmediated presence is possible. When we are gazing at something, we are not doing other things; the gaze is at the forefront of the haze of all possible thoughts, feelings, or actions that we may have, or do, at any given moment. When one gazes that is what is happening with the gazer, at the sacrifice of all else. Now we can and do gaze at many things over the course of a day, a month, or a lifetime. We might consider doing an inventory of our gazes. What would this inventory tell us about ourselves, our desires, our imaginations, and our worlds? Perhaps, some of us do not gaze at anything. That is, an invested attention to anything or anyone is not there. Instead, we may bounce around, noticing more and more things, so that nothing or no one ever is allowed the space and time to dwell with us, truly to have our attention. Maybe, the more there is to gaze upon less gazing will occur.

Gazing as an enduring attentiveness requires discipline and an openness to discovery. After the initial gaze, which is more reflexive and less self-conscious, we might turn our attention away when we get tired, or bored, when we surmise that we have seen and felt all there is to see and to feel. Something else may distract us, enticing us to gaze upon it. If our gaze is always and only the reflex to an object, or to a person, at that initial level of presence, then our gaze will quickly fade or go elsewhere.

Gazing beyond the initial fascination requires commitment; we enter into the realm of the will to see what reality will reveal. We commit to the discovery of the mystery that is the gazer and the gazed upon. The mystery of the Eucharist is approached appropriately with such a gaze, the Eucharistic gaze. The Eucharistic gaze has two modes: gazing on and within the Eucharist, and Eucharistically gazing on everything else. There is an *intra* and *extra* Eucharistic gaze.

The *intra* Eucharistic gaze is not an objective observation but a faithful participation. It is not a study of the Eucharist whereby someone remains detached in order to describe what is happening. The Eucharist is an event of purposeful participation. It is what it is as a gathering of people who recognize that this is where and how they belong, and they are willing to sacrifice for this belonging. The gaze of a faithful participant is an abiding return to what will happen, and who will be present at this Eucharist. The participant returns to what is the same and to what is possible. The abiding structure and economy of the Eucharist provides the recognition, the remembering, that places the participants within the dynamics of revelation. The gaze is an attentive expectation to what and where new life is given. The Eucharistic gaze is an enduring reception of renewal. We do not exhaust the meaning of the Eucharist, because our existence is not in the mode of progressive knowledge exercised by the current codes of human rationality. We must learn the Eucharist from the Eucharist. This learning does not begin without regard for what we have learned already or for our prior habits of learning. However, we enter into a transformation of learning within the Eucharistic way of knowing and of the known. We are not to bring our complete schemes of knowing and meaning to the Eucharist and to its customary questions. The effort of knowing is not to fit the Eucharist into a pre-constructed view of what is real, true, or meaningful. The questions and answers of human discourse and thought cannot be adopted, or even adapted, by Eucharistic thought and discourse without the transformation that occurs within the Eucharist itself. Eucharistic theology has a philosophical dimension and scope without becoming a product of any philosophy.

Likewise, the *intra* Eucharistic gaze does not allow for just the repetition of the questions and of the answers from the tradition(s) of Eucharistic theology. The disposition of reception to renewal is the proper mode of encountering the tradition of the Eucharist and its customary concerns. The Eucharist is an abiding reality within the tradition or past, in the present and in the future. Basically and ultimately, there is no fourth-century, sixteenth-century or twenty-first century Eucharist. There are practices and understandings that characterize these periods, but they do not define or confine the Eucharist. They illuminate the Eucharist. Ideally, they are vestiges of our attempts to speak what we have heard, to depict what we have seen. We gaze at the whole of the tradition as an array of reflections of human fidelity, understanding and imagination of what the Eucharist is and of what happens during its enactment. This does not mean there has never been disagreement and conflict over the Eucharist. I do not propose that we force every view and practice into a predetermined grand narrative. Instead, we need to bring the various theologies, traditions and practices regarding the Eucharist into a framework that is accountable to the wholeness, the catholicity, which the Eucharist grants and implies.

Likewise, I propose that we attend to the whole Eucharist. When pursuing certain theological and liturgical questions customarily posed to the Eucharist, we need to avoid a tightly drawn circle of discourse around one part of this theology or of the liturgy. For example, when pursuing the question of Christ's presence in relation to the bread and wine, we will work within an array of affirmations and understandings of Christ's presence in the world, in the church, and in the celebration of the Eucharist as a whole. While giving due attention to sections and phrases of the Eucharistic prayer, we cannot forget the various claims of Christ's presence in terms of its nature, place, and economy. Where is Christ present? When is Christ present? How is Christ present? And especially, why is Christ present? We will attend to different modes of the encounter between Christ and the baptized within the Eucharist, and how this encounter is mediated by language, action, disposition and materiality. Our understanding of the Eucharist is perceived within a multidimensional totality of texts, actions, materials and intentions. This understanding will not be manufactured within a framework outside of the liturgy itself. Eucharistic questions should not become primarily philosophical, linguistic, sociological, or anthropological ones.

The *extra* Eucharistic gaze is the movement from the Eucharist toward the world. The Eucharist is an event that takes place within the church but the whole world is its horizon. What happens in the Eucharist is for the life of the world. The celebrants, all the baptized, leave the celebration with a Eucharistic mission. This mission has various dimensions. The celebrants are to live Eucharistic lives. They are to invite others into the Eucharistic celebration and life. They are to work towards the realization of a Eucharistic world in the most comprehensive and fullest sense. How we approach the world, how we live in the world and how we define world are to be shaped by the reality we have come to know and share in the Eucharist. We go into the world on a mission derived from our formation as Eucharistic people. It is imperative to acknowledge that we have a mission to the world, to that which is not church. The Eucharist is not only an intra-ecclesial project of whatever sort. There is a tendency to view and to practice the Eucharist for reasons constituted outside of the Eucharist, to gaze on the Eucharist from other places of perception, reality and concerns. These places might be ecclesiastical authority, doctrinal allegiance, community building, cultural awareness, justice seeking, experiential expression, consciousness raising, sensitivity training, and so forth. We can view the Eucharist as a means to another end, however appropriate that end may be or however that end may find a place in the Eucharistic economy. The Eucharistic gaze looks out to the world as a formed view, perception, awareness, and direction. This does not mean that we are not to see how the world actually is, but we are to envision what the world could become as a Eucharistic reality. Presence, peace, offering, giving, sacrifice, forgiveness, reconciliation, remembrance, and narrative are all grand themes of the Eucharist comprising the mission to the world. Again, these themes must be identified from within the Eucharist rather than being adopted from elsewhere. This does not mean that non-Eucharistic discourses cannot assist the articulation and development of these themes, while remaining faithful to the Eucharistic identification and direction inherent within them. Likewise, a proper Eucharistic discourse will address other discourses, the Eucharistic scope of concern and understanding will have cultural, linguistic, philosophical, economic, and political dimensions.

In what follows, I will strive to address Eucharistic questions in Eucharistic ways. This is not a compendium of different views. I have not sought to rehearse the standard arguments and personages of the long history of debate. This work can be viewed as a companion to several other studies on every facet of the history, liturgy, practice, and theology of the Eucharist. The reader can turn to many books worthy of our attention for detailed examinations and representative bibliography. Instead, I will seek to cultivate the Eucharistic gaze both as a movement within, and as a movement without, the event of the Eucharist. This will be done by abiding within the tradition of Eucharistic enactment and understanding, while recognizing the variations and complexities/perplexities presented by it. Along the way, dealing with Eucharistic questions will involve, explicitly and implicitly, the comprehensive scope of other basic theological concepts. Reflection on the Eucharist will take Christological, soteriological, and ecclesiological directions. This is an effort to abide within the Eucharist in the course of reflecting on the customary areas of its exposition, i.e. tradition, presence and sacrifice. However, as has been indicated thus far, the Eucharist is a theologically comprehensive reality and perspective. Thus, we will consider the nature and purpose of the church and of the Christian life from within the Eucharist. Finally, we will take up the question of theology as a proper Eucharistic one.

CHAPTER 1

TRADITION

For I received from the Lord what I also handed on to you, that the Lord Jesus on the night when he was betrayed took a loaf of bread, and when he had given thanks, broke it and said, "This is my body that is for you. Do this in remembrance of me." In the same way he took the cup also, after supper, saying, "This cup is the new covenant in my blood. Do this, as often as you drink it, in remembrance of me." For as often as you eat this bread and drink the cup, you proclaim the Lord's death until he comes.[1]

1 Corinthians 11:23–26

The first account we have of the institution of the Eucharist, and its celebration, is introduced by a reference to tradition. Paul speaks of "receiving from the Lord" and "handing on" what he recounts to the Eucharistic community in Corinth. Reflection on the tradition of the celebration and meaning of the Eucharist begins within that tradition. We do not have sources for the study of the Eucharist that are not mediated by tradition and that are not handed on to us through and as tradition. What is available to us for the study of the origins and development of the Eucharist, its history and theology, are texts that issue from a prior Eucharistic life. While these texts are sources for our study, they are also witnesses of the tradition. They were generated for the sake of continuing and/or explaining what the church was already doing. The sources for study of the Eucharist, and this is particularly the case prior to the Reformation, are ways of "handing on" what is being done. The sources are not attempts to create a Eucharist where one does not exist. These are witnesses to various faithful attempts to "hand-on" what has been "received from the

Lord." Our approach to these texts should remain mindful of how we abide faithfully within the continuum of receiving and handing-on. We engage the tradition within its characteristic dynamic of receiving from others what we will hand-on to others. We have to learn what we will teach, and this learning and teaching occurs within a shared life shaped by the enactment of our subject.

Because the textual witness to the tradition issues from a Eucharistic life, it does not tell us everything about this life. Our sources come from a variety of contexts and circumstances, each bearing a theological rationale that is not completely or definitively articulated. This means that we should exercise some modesty in our claims and conclusions we draw from the study of the Eucharistic tradition. As witnesses to the tradition, the texts serve as sources both of what is being handed on and of what is received. This exchange of giving and receiving is an enduring dynamic that requires that we do not attempt to construct a linear story of the development of the Eucharist. There will be gaps in our understanding, and we should not yield to the temptation to cover them over with heavily footnoted speculation. Perhaps, the recognition of the incompleteness of the Eucharistic tradition will guide us into a deeper sense of the nature of the Eucharist itself.

In this chapter, I will not present a survey of the history of the celebration and theology of the Eucharist. Rather, I will attend to what the historical sources tell us about the nature and development of the tradition of the Eucharist. I will approach these documents as witnesses to the Eucharistic tradition, and not as sources for historical reconstruction of the celebration and meaning of the Eucharist. My main concern is how the documents reflect an understanding and practice of the Eucharist that we receive. Put another way, the emphasis here is not on what generated the texts, but on what the texts can generate. We want to keep alive the question of tradition and not bury it under mounds of definitive or contested readings. The questions of what happened, and what did it mean, are asked for the sake of what can happen, and what it can mean? We should ask what is being handed on to us, and what can it mean?

FIRST WITNESSES

We began with a quotation from Paul's first letter to the Corinthians because it gives us our first written account of what is customarily referred to as the "institution narrative." There are four of these narratives of Jesus' words at the Last Supper. In addition to the Corinthians account, there is one in each of the synoptic Gospels: Matthew (26: 26–28), Mark (14:22–24), and Luke (22:17–20). All these are called "institution narratives" because with words and actions they describe how Jesus is said to have instituted the Eucharist. As I have noted, the institution narrative in First Corinthians is conveyed through appeal to tradition, to a prior teaching and life. Also, Paul wrote to a community already engaged in the regular celebration of the Eucharist. The recounting of this narrative serves to reenforce Paul's admonition toward appropriate Eucharistic practice. He appeals to tradition in order to address a contemporary situation. What about the renditions found in the synoptic Gospels? Are they too witnesses to tradition, rather than originators of that tradition? The answer to this question is complicated and can vary. Suffice it to say at this point that the Gospels were written by persons and within communities already involved in the regular celebration of the Eucharist. The Eucharist preceded the Gospels. We do not have the institution of the Eucharist without the emerging tradition of the Eucharist. Therefore, we will consider these institution narratives as first witnesses to the Eucharistic tradition. Each of the four narratives will be examined individually and then will be compared with each other. After this examination and comparison, the question of tradition will be posed directly.

Prior to considering the narratives in turn, we would do well to bracket for now our experiences of those narratives as found within Eucharistic prayers. We can be so accustomed to hearing and seeing them as focal points of our Eucharistic prayers we might not pay close attention to their distinctiveness. The place, wording, and use of the institution narratives in the New Testament are not the same as found in most Eucharistic prayers. This caveat of distinction between the first witnesses and later Eucharistic prayers holds not only for textual analysis, but also for theological attribution. Witnesses to the tradition are not the same as proof-texts for well-established theological viewpoints.

Paul's version of the institution narrative, which he "hands on" to the Corinthians, locates the Supper "on the night" Jesus was betrayed. Jesus takes a loaf of bread and gives thanks before breaking it, and he states that the bread "is my body that is for you." The memorial injunction is added: "Do this is in remembrance of me." The actions and words with the cup occur "after supper" and "in the same way." The cup is called "the new covenant in my blood." The memorial injunction is added here as well. A meal takes place between the bread and cup.

Before the actions and words with the bread and cup, Luke relates that Jesus gathered the apostles at the table, and he spoke of desiring to eat the Passover with them, adding, "I will not eat it until it is fulfilled in the kingdom of God." Then Jesus takes a cup, gives thanks, and tells the apostles to take it and distribute it among themselves. He tells them he will not "drink of the fruit of the vine until the kingdom of God comes." Next, he takes a loaf of bread, gives thanks, breaks it, and gives it to the apostles, saying, "This is my body, which is given for you. Do this in remembrance of me." After supper, Jesus takes a cup in the same way that he took the bread, and says, "This cup that is poured out for you is the new covenant in my blood." There is no memorial injunction for the cup. While Luke has the bread and cup actions and words separated by a meal, as does Paul, his account differs from Paul's in two ways: Luke places the cup before the bread, and he attaches the memorial injunction only to the bread. Luke and Paul both speak of the cup as the new covenant in Jesus' blood, and Luke continues with "poured out for you."

Mark's recension of the institution narrative places the words and actions with bread "while they were eating." Jesus blesses, breaks, and gives the bread, saying "Take; this is my body." Then Jesus takes a cup and gives thanks, and the disciples receive it and drink from it. He tells them, "This is my blood of the covenant which is poured out for many." He continues with "I will never again drink it new in the kingdom of God." Mark's version does not have a meal between the bread and cup nor the memorial injunction. He places Jesus' words regarding the future drinking in the kingdom of God after the cup while Luke has them before the bread and cup. In Mark, Jesus "blesses" the bread and "gives thanks" over the cup.

The institution narrative in Matthew is almost identical to the one in Mark. Matthew has "eat" in the words distributing the bread and adds "for the forgiveness of sins" to the words over the cup. While Mark has the disciples drinking from the cup, Matthew has Jesus directing them to do so. Like Mark, Matthew places the narrative during the meal and concludes with the saying of not drinking wine again until the "Father's kingdom" (instead of Mark's "kingdom of God"). There is no memorial injunction on either bread or cup.

What can these four versions of the institution narrative tell us about the tradition of the Eucharist? First, they allow us to identify two traditions: Mark/Matthew and Paul/Luke. Mark and Matthew share significant differences compared to Luke and Paul. Both lack the memorial injunction, while Paul has it for the bread and cup and Luke for the bread. Likewise, Mark and Matthew locate the narrative during the meal. Paul and Luke have the meal between the bread and the cup. In Mark and Matthew, Jesus "blesses" the bread whereas in Luke and Paul, he "gives thanks." Luke and Paul add "for you" to the words over the bread, while Mark and Matthew do not. Also, Luke and Paul refer to the "new covenant" where Mark and Matthew have "covenant." Mark and Matthew speak of the "blood poured out" and Luke of the "cup that is poured out." Paul does not have this phrase, but he alone has "proclaim the Lord's death until he comes." The symmetry between the bread and cup words in Mark/Matthew suggests liturgical shaping. That is, through liturgical recitation, the account takes on more of a ritual expression than a personal statement. Likewise, the absence of the intervening meal between the bread and cup could reflect a practice whereby the meal preceded the Eucharist. Or, as occurred in a later development, the Eucharist might have already been celebrated without a meal. The Mark/Matthew tradition does not have the memorial injunction. Was it added later, or was it not considered necessary because the act enjoined was being performed?

Reflecting on these two traditions does not determine finally what really were the words of Jesus at the Last Supper. Nor can we say definitively which account is more primitive. While Paul is dated the earliest text, this does not mean that it represents the earliest tradition. Matthew is dependent on Mark as a whole, which could explain the strong similarity between their accounts of the Last Supper. Complicating matters further, what about the first cup in Luke? Why do some manuscripts of this Gospel not have the second cup? Was the Last Supper a Passover meal (Synoptics), or did it occur on the day before Passover (John)? These historical-critical questions are not my chief concern. One can find well-documented arguments on all sides of each question. Instead, I am asking how can we appreciate these accounts as witnesses to the emerging Eucharistic tradition(s) of the church.

The way to begin to do this is to acknowledge that the institution narrative, whether located within the passion story or directly within the church's life, is itself shaped by preceding tradition. What Jesus did and said at the Last Supper regarding bread and wine was unique. However, the structure and nature of the institution narrative, what is done and what it means, has been "handed on" from the Jewish liturgical tradition. Jesus and the early church act out of the Jewish liturgical tradition while establishing the Christian Eucharistic tradition.

The Last Supper was not the first meal Jesus had with his disciples. The Gospels attest to Jesus and his disciples sharing meals, sometimes with thousands, and we can presume that they ate together on an almost daily basis. Also, as faithful Jews, Jesus and the disciples kept the Jewish festive meal tradition on the designated holy days. The Last Supper, whether it was the Passover meal or a meal with Passover implications, reflects the liturgical tradition of the festive home meal. This meal began with thanksgiving over the first cup, followed by the head of the family blessing a loaf of bread, breaking it, and sharing it with those in attendance. This breaking of bread began the meal proper. After the meal, the final cup of wine was blessed and shared. The presider at this meal would pray according to tradition but not according to a prescribed and fixed text. Certain themes would be present: blessing of God for creation, thanksgiving for the redemptive acts of God, and a petition for God's mercy anew, looking toward the future. However, the presider would incorporate into this prayer the occasion for gathering, a particular theme marking the day.

We can see that the account of the Last Supper in Luke resembles more closely the ritual structure of the Jewish festive meal. Does this mean that Luke is the most primitive account? Or, that both Paul and Luke reflect an earlier stratum of the tradition because they retain the intervening meal? It is impossible to reach definitive answers to these questions. Literary conformity is not necessarily the same as historical origination. What we can say is that the Eucharistic tradition emerged from the Jewish liturgical tradition. The primitive Eucharistic tradition retained the structure of blessing and thanksgiving over bread and wine, the sense of being gathered together through the sharing of a meal, and a prayer that is both traditional and extemporaneous. Likewise, the themes of creation, redemption, and petition are found in developing Eucharistic prayers.

EARLY WITNESSES

The emergence of the Eucharistic tradition from the Jewish table tradition is evident in the first textual witness we have of the Eucharistic life of early Christians. The *Didache*, a document from Syria, dated anywhere from the end of the first century to the beginning of the second century, gives us our first Eucharistic texts after the New Testament.[2] These texts are found in chapters 9, 10, and 14. However, it is important to appreciate the document as a whole in order to gain an appropriate sense of the Eucharistic celebration within the church's life. The *Didache* belongs to a category of early Christian documents called "Church Orders." They contain a variety of texts, teachings, and directions for the church's liturgical and moral life.

The *Didache* begins with six chapters of teaching on the two ways: life and death. This is followed by instruction for performing baptisms. The Eucharistic material comes after baptism. An important recognition here is that the Eucharist is both the central act of the baptized and a part of a greater whole. It is the focal point but not in isolation. Turning directly to these texts, the prayers in chapters 9 and 10, there is an ongoing scholarly debate whether what we have here are Eucharistic prayers proper or prayers for an agape meal. The problem of assessing chapters 9 and 10 is made difficult if we have an a priori view of what Eucharistic prayers are supposed to be. There is always the temptation to read the tradition backward rather than forward. For example, these prayers do not have the institution narrative, which we expect to find in every Eucharistic prayer. The prayers in chapters 9 and 10 reflect the structure of Jewish table prayers with the distinct sections of blessing, while reshaping the content in light of Jesus. I will not enter into the debate whether they are strictly Eucharistic prayers or not. Instead, I will consider these prayers for what they communicate about a Eucharistic perspective on the Christian life.

Chapter 9 contains prayers for use first over the cup and then over broken bread. Both prayers begin with thanksgiving to the Father for the revelation made through Jesus. The cup is "the holy vine of your child David," and the gratitude expressed for the bread is "for the life and knowledge." These prayers are introduced with the directive: "About the thanksgiving: give thanks thus." The prayers and accompanying actions are called "thanksgiving" as well in the directive at the end of the chapter, stating that only the baptized are allowed to eat and drink this cup and bread. The Christian life is centered on thanksgiving to God for what has been revealed in Jesus, who is the "child" or "servant" of the Father. Baptism is entry into this life of thanksgiving and knowledge. Baptism is also a life of being gathered with all the baptized at the table. The third section of chapter 9 is a petition that as scattered bread is made one so may the church be gathered from "the ends of the earth into your kingdom." Thanksgiving made through the cup and bread for what God has revealed places the baptized into a movement toward each other as they are drawn closer to God's kingdom.

Chapter 10 begins with the instruction: "And after you have had your fill give thanks thus." The prayer is characterized by thanksgiving to God, the Father, "for the knowledge and faith and immortality" revealed in Jesus, and for creation, especially food and drink. The prayer then emphasizes God's gift of spiritual food and drink along with eternal life "through your child Jesus." The last line of the second section reads: "Above all we give you thanks because you are mighty; glory to you for evermore." While thanks is given for what God has done in creation and through Jesus, the prayer does not lose sight of the ultimate reality of God. We give thanks to God for who God is and not just for what God has done, and can do, for us. Similar to the prayer in chapter 9, the third section is a prayer for the church. God is asked to "remember" the church so as to rid it of evil and bring it to perfection through God's love. God is asked to gather the whole church "from the four winds" into God's kingdom. The prayer concludes with a call for the Lord to come and bring this fulfillment of the kingdom. Thanksgiving leads to expectation and not to stagnation. Thanksgiving offered to God yields a desire that God and God's kingdom become everything. That is, thanksgiving is not limited to what God has placed within our lives. Rather, this thanksgiving reveals where and how God is drawing us into the fullness and comprehensiveness of what God desires for us.

Chapter 14 of the *Didache* is instruction regarding the Eucharist proper. When Christians come together on the Lord's Day to give thanks and break bread, they are to prepare themselves through the confession of their sins and through reconciliation with their "companions." The Eucharist requires an honest and direct engagement with the disorder of our interior life and with our common life with others. We do not enter into God's movement of thanksgiving, expectation, and reconciliation through Jesus, unless we are willing to face the absence of this movement within ourselves and among the baptized.

Written in Rome about the year 150 AD, as an effort to defuse the notion that Christians are dangerous to the social order, Justin's *First Apology* gives us the first account of a complete Eucharist. Justin describes a Eucharist after a baptism (chapter 65) and on a typical Sunday (chapter 67), and he provides a theological summary of the Eucharist (chapter 66). He does not provide a detailed picture of the Eucharist but an outline of what happened. Combining the two accounts, Justin tells us the following:

> And on the day called Sunday an assembly is held in one place of all who live in town or country, and the records of the apostles or the writings of the prophets are read as time allows. (67)
>
> Then, when the reader has finished, the president in a discourse admonishes and exhorts (us) to imitate these good things. (67)
>
> Then we all stand up together and send up prayers; and as we said before, when we have finished praying, bread and wine and water are brought up, and the president likewise sends up prayers and thanksgivings to the best of his ability, and people assent, saying Amen; (67)
>
> Then bread and a cup of water and (a cup) of mixed wine are brought to him who presides over the brethren, and he takes them and sends up praise and glory to the Father of all in the name of the Son and of the Holy Spirit, and gives thanks at some length that we have been deemed worthy of these things from him. When he has finished the prayers and the thanksgiving, all the people give their assent by saying "Amen." (65)
>
> And the (elements over which) thanks have been given are distributed, and everyone partakes; and they are sent through the deacons to those who are not present. (67)

No longer do we have a meal attached to, or incorporated within, a Eucharistic gathering. The Eucharist begins with readings from what will be deemed the Old and New Testaments, and they are followed by a homily. Then the "prayers of the people" lead to the offering. After the prayers, chapter 65 has the kiss of peace. The Eucharistic prayer is not a set text but something the president prays extemporaneously according to expected theological themes. We do not know whether the institution narrative was a normative part of this prayer. Justin does refer to the institution narrative as a warrant for the performance of the Eucharist.

> For the apostles in the records composed by them which are called gospels, have handed down thus what was commanded of them: that Jesus took bread, gave thanks, and said, "Do this for the remembrance of me; this is my body;" and likewise he took the cup, gave thanks, and said "This is my blood;" and gave to them alone. (66)

What we have here is the basic shape of the Eucharist that will abide throughout the tradition. This structure becomes the way we recognize the economy of the Eucharist, the way it moves and works. As witnesses to the tradition become more numerous, expansive, and complex, Justin's outline provides the way to map the landscape of what changes and what gets obscured and confusing. Unless an event matches the basic actions given here, this event is not a Eucharist. However, we might have a description or prescription of a Eucharist in which these basic actions are difficult to identify or have been so laden with interpretive commentary that the original simplicity and economy of the whole action is neglected or underappreciated.

The next witness we have of the Eucharistic tradition is a Church Order known as *The Apostolic Tradition* of Hippolytus (c.215). This document provides important contributions to our understanding of baptism, ordinations, and the Eucharist. It has been influential in the development of Eucharistic tradition both in the past and in the present. Versions of the *Apostolic Tradition* are found in other early liturgical documents, and it was a model for many liturgical revisions, including revisions of the Eucharistic prayer, during the twentieth century. Originally written in Greek and located in Rome, it exists in several manuscripts in a variety of translations. Our focus on this witness is twofold: what it tells us about the emerging Eucharistic tradition, and particularly, what it tells us about the Eucharistic prayer.

Hippolytus begins his exposition of the liturgical practices in Rome with a prologue giving the reason for this work. He intends to convey the tradition that should be maintained by the church and its leaders. Having received the tradition from this treatise, the leaders "may hold fast to that tradition which has continued until now." Furthermore, leaders are to teach this tradition in opposition to "apostasy or error" that is being taught and practiced by others. Here we have a witness to tradition that is not just a "handing on" but a defense of previous teaching and performance over against newer and different forms of liturgical celebration and understanding. The expression and articulation of tradition has become, and does so more and more through the church's history, an exercise in differentiation and argument. The "appeal" to tradition can objectify its existence so that the "receiving" of what is "handed on" becomes an attempt to maintain the tradition through the imitation of forms. The context of the receivers is supplanted by the formative context of what is being handed on.

It is surprising, then, that when treating the Eucharistic prayer, Hippolytus reflects the tradition by not offering a fixed and immutable form. He provides the first instance of what we would unambiguously designate a Eucharistic prayer. The prayer is given as an example of what a newly ordained bishop might pray at his ordination Eucharist. While Hippolytus articulates a complete text, he does not insist that it be followed. In a later chapter, he writes:

> And the bishop shall give thanks according to what we said above. It is not at all necessary for him to utter the same words that we said above, as though reciting them from memory, when giving thanks to God; but let each pray according to his ability. If indeed he is able to pray sufficiently and with a solemn prayer, it is good. But if anyone who prays, recites a prayer according to a fixed form, do not prevent him. Only, he must pray what is sound and orthodox. (Chapter 9:3–5)

Remaining within the tradition is not so much the repetition of immutable texts but the ongoing expression of the church's faith. Tradition is not ultimately a matter of how something is spoken or handed on, but what matters is what is spoken or handed on. The exhortation to Eucharistic fidelity—"Do this in remembrance of me"—is fulfilled by a keeping of memory that does not require, and may even exclude, imitation. For Hippolytus, the fixed form is secondary and serves a purpose that transcends the language itself. The language is accountable to a theological and Eucharistic life that is represented by the prayer but not bound by it. The tradition of Eucharistic praying will become more and more identified with precise and repetitious language, while becoming disconnected from theological exposition.

The Eucharistic prayer found in *The Apostolic Tradition* has the following structure: opening dialogue; thanksgiving to God for the sending and redemptive work of Jesus; institution narrative; remembering and offering; request for the sending of the Holy Spirit upon the offering; and concluding doxology. Part of the usual structure of subsequent Eucharistic prayers that is not found here is the Sanctus. Yet, the structure and dynamic of this prayer is found in many Eucharistic prayers that emerge in the fourth century and later. This indicates that a normative understanding and expectation of what constitutes a Eucharistic prayer, and how it theologically works, is developing. The tradition is becoming more substantive and prescriptive. However, the tradition of Eucharistic praying does not become singular and absolute. Other structures and theological dynamics appear and form various types of Eucharistic prayers. A sense of this variety can be gained by looking at another Eucharistic prayer that originated prior to the fourth century.

The *Liturgy of Saints Addai and Mari* appears as an eccentricity to perceptions honed by familiarity with contemporary Western Eucharistic prayers. Composed in Syriac and originating from East Syria, a manuscript of this liturgy was found in Mosul, Iraq in 1928. The manuscript is dated around the tenth or eleventh century, but scholarly consensus holds that it reflects a "primitive" Eucharistic prayer from the third century. Scholars of this liturgy employ various strategies to remove sections of the prayer thought to be later additions. One such strategy is comparing *Addai and Mari* to the Eucharistic prayer known as the *Third Anaphora of Saint Peter*, which contains portions of it. Along with the prayers of *Theodore the Interpreter* and *Nestorius*, they form a group of Eucharistic prayers classified as "East Syrian."

The most striking feature of *Addai and Mari* is the absence of the institution narrative. It does contain a line that speaks of receiving the form commanded by Jesus; however, whether or not this refers to the institution narrative is debated. The Holy Spirit is invoked to "bless and sanctify" the offering of those gathered to the end that their sins are forgiven, with hope for the resurrection of the dead and the kingdom of heaven. All extant manuscripts include a Sanctus, after the first section devoted to praise of the Holy Trinity and intercessions. Scholarly reconstruction of an earlier edition of the prayer removes the Sanctus and intercessions, considering them later additions. The prayer has a structure similar to the Jewish pattern of a series of blessings, which also indicates a "primitive" character. This is in contrast to later prays, as well as the *Apostolic Tradition*, which proceed more like a linear narrative.

The existence and study of *Addai and Mari* reveals some salient points regarding the nature of the developing Eucharistic tradition. One is that access to the tradition comes from and through the tradition. We do not have the original text of the prayer, nor do we know whether such a text was prescriptive or descriptive. One scholarly treatment of the manuscripts is the peeling off layers that were added, as the prayer was used in different contexts and periods of the church's Eucharistic life. Often study of the tradition is dealing with what was received as the way to reflect on what was handed on. Another point is that the church did not settle on one normative structure for the Eucharistic prayer. Different structures developed in different places and at different times. We should reject any attempt to make all of these prayers fit into an explanatory schema imposed on them from a time, place, and perspective that they did not originally share. A final point *Addai and Mari* highlights is the margins of tradition. The prayer is discovered in South India and Iraq, and is used by Nestorian Christians. When attending to the Eucharistic tradition, we should not just focus on the liturgical and theological centers of the church. We should also cast our view at the margins. We cannot narrow our view to what has been handed on by only looking at what we have received: the "we" being circumscribed by denomination, culture, geography, and doctrine.

NORMATIVE WITNESSES

The fourth century is a paradigmatic period for the history of liturgy and for the Eucharist in particular. Two major dynamics shaped the development and the expansion of the rites of baptism and Eucharist: the legalization, later authorization, of Christianity by the state, and the theological controversies leading to the Councils of Nicea and Constantinople. When the church became a public institution, its worship moved from houses to buildings. The performance of the Eucharist in large spaces affected the rite by incorporating processions and adapting state court ceremonial. An additional factor was the attendance of large numbers of people. The ceremonial of the Eucharist became more elaborate and expanded, including Eucharistic prayers. Stimulated by controversy, broadened and deepened by creative theologians, the Christian faith was increasingly expressed in more sophisticated and authoritative ways. Questions of the nature and person of Jesus, of the oneness of God, and of the Holy Spirit, were pursued with a vigor we might find surprising. The theological life of the church entered a formative stage that would become a standard for all subsequent Christian teaching and identity.

Any study of the history and development of the Eucharist that aspires to be in any way comprehensive will give a substantial amount of attention to the fourth century. In addition to the changes in ceremonial, this was the time when important textual and theological progression of Eucharistic prayers occurred. A variety of Eucharistic prayers that were employed regularly appear in the tradition. The liturgy was undergoing a transition that included movement from extemporaneous to written Eucharistic prayers. It is a movement from praying the tradition to praying traditional texts. The Eucharistic tradition became something primarily handed on by texts rather than by directives: more by "go and say" than "go and do." The fourth century saw the inauguration of this movement. These texts are much lengthier and theologically richer than what we have considered thus far, and in fact seem extravagant compared with many of our more concise and sober contemporary Eucharistic prayers. Some of these prayers are being used by Eastern Orthodox Churches as well as in an adapted version in some Western Churches. Also, these prayers have helped to shape other Eucharistic prayers developed at other stages in the tradition. Thus, after the fourth century, we can begin to speak of normative witnesses to the Eucharistic tradition.

Scholarly engagement with fourth century Eucharistic prayers classifies them into four "families" primarily based on their respective structures. These families are: West Syrian (Antiochene), East Syrian, Egyptian (Alexandrian), and Roman. Prior to a closer examination of the structural nature and variety of these families, I will provide a working understanding of the customary sections that constitute Eucharistic prayers. Again, this is an imposed schema from analysis of texts and not an outline that the author followed in producing them. All Eucharistic prayers begin with some form of dialogue between the presider and the people. This exchange leads the presider to continue with a praise and blessing of God for who God is and for what God has done. This initial section concludes with the Sanctus (Holy, Holy, Holy…), which begins to appear in the prayers of the fourth century. After the Sanctus (usually referred to as the post-Sanctus section), a prayer of thanksgiving focused on God's redemptive acts fulfilled in Jesus Christ was often prayed. This thanksgiving-redemption section culminates with the institution narrative. The command "Do this in remembrance of me" is taken up by an articulation of what is remembered about Jesus, particularly his death and resurrection. This section is called "memorial" or *anamnesis*. Remembering Jesus and his salvific events marks a significant transition in the prayer from attention to who God is, and what God has done, to supplication to God for what God can do now and in the future. The supplication or petition begins with the offering of the "gifts" of bread and wine, and may include the offering of the believers themselves. The movement toward God is initiated by oblation. The offering and offered self ask God to act in ways that reflect how God has acted already and to continue those ways for which they have responded with thanksgiving. Offering is followed by invocation or *epiclesis*. God is asked to send the Holy Spirit onto the gifts so that they become the body and blood of Christ. The Holy Spirit is also invoked over the people so that they may be sanctified and united. These two *epicleses* are designated consecratory (over the gifts) and communion (over the people). The supplication section of the prayer is often supplemented with a series of intercessions: petitions to God on behalf of the church, the sick and departed, the government, and the world. The language of petition varies, and given the place of the intercessions within the Eucharistic prayer, they can be regarded as extensions of the *epiclesis*. That is, the scope and effect of the work of the Holy Spirit thus invoked is given hopeful expression. The prayer concludes with a doxology, praise offered to the Triune God sharing in God's eternal life.

The structure and the economy of the Eucharistic prayer just described are characteristic of the West Syrian family. Examples of this group include the *Liturgies of St. James, St. Basil, and St. John Chrysostom* as well as several prayers in the 1979 *Book of Common Prayer* of the Episcopal Church. Not every prayer in this family includes intercessions, as is the case of the prayer in the *Apostolic Tradition* of Hippolytus. This West Syrian schema introduces the basic dimensions of the Eucharistic prayer, and the theological rationale implicit within it. The word or concept of "dimension" is chosen instead of "part" or its equivalent, because it suggests a more adequate appreciation of the Eucharistic prayer as a proper theological text, as language offered to God for God's own use. A dimension can only be assessed in view of all the other dimensions. A dimension gives a sense of the whole, while not reducing the whole to it. Dimensions lead one to a greater awareness of the whole, and yet this awareness is available through the particular dimension. A part of the whole can be, or often is, understood on its own terms; one can embrace a theology of the part rather than of the whole. We can construct a series of self-enclosed understandings for each part and then collect them to form a theology of the whole. For example, we can have an understanding of what the institution narrative does, or what happens during the *epiclesis*, but we might not draw out the mutuality between them, or include reference to the concluding doxology as the horizon from which light is cast on these dimensions illuminating the whole prayer as an arena for God's encounter with the baptized gathered for the Eucharist.

The East Syrian family of Eucharistic prayers resembles the West Syrian except the intercessions come before the *epiclesis* instead of after it. The most complete representative of this family is the *Third Anaphora of St. Peter*, which was mentioned above regarding its commonality with *Addai and Mari*. Similar to other Eucharistic prayers that have their origins in the fourth century, this prayer is expansive and theologically untidy compared to many contemporary Eucharistic prayers. It shows us that the familiar dimensions of a Eucharistic prayer can be present in unfamiliar ways. Two examples will be offered: the institution narrative and the intercessions. This prayer does not contain an intact version of the institution narrative drawn directly from the New Testament. Instead, we find a mix of phrases from the synoptics, Paul's "proclaim the Lord's death until he comes," and the Johannine phrases "I am the living bread" along with "for the life of the world." What is missing, and what we would expect to find, is the injunction "Do this in remembrance of me." The institution narrative section is introduced by: "We make the memorial of your Passion, Lord, as you taught us." Repetition of the command is not necessary for its obedience. Here is fidelity to the will of Jesus that is not exclusively performed by the recitation of the directive phrase. Eucharistic fidelity to the memory of Jesus is not ultimately constituted by the utterances of approved formulae. Yet, Eucharistic fidelity to the memory of Jesus will be recognizable as such. All of the Eucharistic language of Jesus is given, is handed on, to those who are keeping memory of him. Who Jesus is, and what has happened to, in, and through him, is anamnetically available to the Eucharistic assembly. Remembering Jesus is sharing in his memory of God and of world: his perspective, knowledge, life, and will. We participate in his memory through fidelity to his nature and will. Thus fidelity is expressed and performed by language that is recognizable without being repetitious. The handing on of the Eucharist, its presentation as tradition, is to be received; it is performed as tradition, so that the Eucharist abides as a recognizable event without exact repetition of its particulars. Recognition of the memory of Jesus, and not the repetition of secondary particular actions and specific words, is a criterion of authentic tradition.

Remembering Jesus as participation in his memory, of what things would look like if lived in him and for him, is portrayed by the intercessions in the *Third Anaphora of St. Peter*. Each petition begins with the phrase "Remember, Lord God, at this time..." The first petition is comprehensive, asking God to remember "the troubled, the afflicted, and those who are in various difficulties." This is followed by petitions for members of the church, for the offerers of sacrifices, for those communicating at this Eucharist. The intercessions conclude with a petition for the presider and for the author of the prayer: that their sins be forgiven. Eucharistic memorial can thus have two directions: past and future, both shaping the present. There is the keeping of memory that recalls all that God has done for God's people, culminating in the person and act of Jesus. The past is brought to the present. In the intercessions, memorial becomes supplication asking God to remember so that the present, "at this time," becomes charged with the possibilities God's presence in Christ entails. Our remembrance of God's salvific acts, including creation, turns toward God's memory of us, and how change can happen within the divine arena of memorial.

This East Syrian family of Eucharistic prayers invokes the Holy Spirit as the final supplication, the divine person of change who comes with the promise of fulfillment. Both the West and East Syrian families join the intercessions to the *epiclesis*; one has the *epiclesis* before and the other after the intercessions. We need to attend to the invocation of the Holy Spirit as the context for the articulation of our desires for God among us. The Eucharistic prayer focuses and intensifies our understanding of who we are, and what we seek, within our Eucharistic relationship to God; what we seek is God's Eucharistic presence for us.

The third family of Eucharistic prayers has its provenance in Egypt, especially Alexandria. Our sources for this group include fragments on papyrus, a Coptic text written on a tablet, and five medieval manuscripts containing the later and complete *Liturgy of St. Mark*. Study of these sources reveals a prayer that developed in stages whereby sections were added through its use over time and through the influence of other Eucharistic prayers. The earliest of these sources is known as The Strasbourg Papyrus; it was written sometime in the fourth or fifth century, but edited and published only in 1928. In the Strasbourg Papyrus, the first part of the prayer is absent, and the text begins with thanksgiving for creation leading to a transition from offering to intercessions: "we offer the reasonable sacrifice and this bloodless service" and "over this sacrifice and offering we pray and beseech you, remember your holy and only Catholic Church, all your peoples and all your flocks." The intercessions, and the text, conclude with a doxology.

Scholarly discussion of this document centers on whether we can designate it a complete Eucharistic prayer or not. It is dominated by offering and intercessory language, while bereft of an institution narrative or an *epiclesis*. Could this be an early Eucharistic prayer that later became the basis for adding what developed as characteristic sections, or normative dimensions, to an anaphora? This seems to be the case. A later source, the British Museum Tablet, written in Coptic, contains a text of a Eucharistic prayer following the Sanctus. Where the Strasbourg papyrus had a doxology, this document now has the Sanctus. The text begins with an invocation: "fill, O God, this sacrifice also with the blessing from you through your Holy Spirit." This "fill" invocation is characteristic of the *Liturgy of St. Mark* and the Egyptian prayers. We can call it a preparatory *epiclesis*, for it introduces the institution narrative. The narrative here is not the culmination of thanksgiving for redemption, as is the case in West Syrian prayers, but is placed within the movement of supplication. The Pauline addition of proclaiming the Lord's death is taken up as a type of memorial. Instead of remembering the mighty acts of salvation, the prayer speaks of proclaiming Christ's death, confessing the resurrection and ascension, and anticipating his second coming. The gifts of bread and wine are then presented and the Holy Spirit is invoked over them to "make" them into the body and blood of Christ. This three-phased movement after the institution narrative— proclaiming (remembering), offering (presenting), invoking—is also found in the West Syrian structure. The final form of the anaphora of the *Liturgy of St. Mark* is greatly expanded compared to earlier sources but retains the basic structure of the Egyptian type. The intercessions are before the Sanctus, there is a "fill" *epiclesis* prior to the institution narrative, and the consecratory *epiclesis* after the presentation of the gifts before God.

We can be so struck by the differences among these families of Eucharistic prayers that we do not attend closely to what is common. The distinctions we notice and draw among traditions, which grew more pronounced as the centuries increase, can garner all of our attention, leaving us in different Eucharistic places. We can stand our ground in different churches and not look for a common Eucharistic ground on which to meet. An abiding question is where do we see the continuities and the scope of the Eucharistic tradition as a whole?

The fourth normative tradition of Eucharistic prayers emerging from the fourth century is Roman. What comes to be known as the Roman Canon is attested to in writings from the end of the fourth century, with complete manuscripts dating from the eighth century. While we can compare structures of the other families according to the location of the intercessions and *epiclesis*, and thereby determine how they arrange the customary dimensions of a Eucharistic prayer, this strategy cannot be used with the Roman Canon. This is a prayer unlike any other, with its closet relative being those in the Egyptian family. Except for the opening dialogue and concluding doxology, its structure does not resemble the prayer in the *Apostolic Tradition* even though it shares a Roman provenance. The Roman Canon consists of a series of short sections, each of which is referred to by its opening Latin words. The institution narrative (*Qui pridie*) is not placed at the conclusion of a thanksgiving section, as is the case with prayers in the West Syrian pattern. However, similar to other families, the institution narrative of the Roman Canon is followed by a transitional section (*Unde et memores*) that moves from remembering to offering. The dominant theme of the prayer is offering and sacrifice, including the way the intercessions appear. Remembering and offering are intertwined throughout the prayer.

One glaring omission from the Roman Canon is an *epiclesis*: It does not have an explicit invocation of the Holy Spirit over the gifts or over the people. The closest thing to an *epiclesis* is the section (*Quam oblationem*) just prior to the institution narrative: "Vouchsafe, we beseech you, O God, to make this offering wholly blessed, approved, ratified, reasonable, and acceptable; that it may become to us the body and blood of your dearly beloved Son Jesus Christ our Lord." Having this petition introduce the institution narrative might indicate that the moment of consecration, when the bread and wine are changed into the body and blood, occurs during the recitation of Jesus' words from the Last Supper in this liturgical form. Indeed, a standard theological understanding associating the consecration of the elements with the rehearsal of the Supper narrative did develop. What of other Eucharistic prayers that assign the "moment" of consecration to the invocation of the Holy Spirit? And to complicate things a little more, what about Eucharistic prayers that do not have the institution narrative (*Addai and Mari*) or an *epiclesis* (1662 English *Book of Common Prayer*)? Are there different ways that bread and wine become the body and blood, or does this happen only by the recitation of the institution narrative or by the *epiclesis*, such that in its textual absence no consecration takes place? These questions surrounding the nature of consecration were hotly debated later in the tradition, and they are the subject of the next chapter. For now, I am drawing attention to the relationship between the text of a Eucharistic prayer and the theological understanding it fosters.

The Roman Canon was prayed during the same centuries that a doctrine of the real presence of Christ in the bread and wine enacted through the recitation of the institution narrative developed and was authorized. Various liturgical practices and pieties associated with the Eucharistic prayer reinforced this doctrine. Likewise, a doctrine of Eucharistic sacrifice, that the Eucharist was a redemptive offering to God, accompanied the expansion and singular use of the Roman Canon in the West. The liturgical tradition of the Roman Canon affected, if not effected, the Eucharistic theological tradition in the West. Eucharistic prayers that became normative in the East, with their consecratory language located with the *epiclesis*, led to a theology of consecration through the action of the Holy Spirit. Certainly, there were theological factors at play between the West and the East that shaped the distinctive emphases on the institution narrative and the *epiclesis*. Yet, the use of different liturgical traditions preceded full-fledged speculative traditions. The Eucharistic liturgy grants an opportunity for understanding or meaning to arise and evolve. This sense of meaning can then stimulate speculative questions, whose pursuit of answers is driven by the concerns and methodologies of non-liturgical arenas of knowing. The text of the prayer asks that the bread and wine become the body and blood of Christ, and this happens when Christ's words are spoken. What does this mean? How do things change from one reality to another? What makes a thing real or true? What are our resources for answering these questions, and how can they help us to make sense of what we pray and believe?

Our understanding of what happens in the Eucharist can, and often has, become separated from the liturgy. The text and performance of a Eucharistic prayer can evoke the search for understanding, and then this search takes on a reality of its own. We can arrive at understandings, speculative constructs, that are not Eucharistic understandings; they cease to emerge from the liturgy, to be an exercise in contemplation of divine mysteries. That is, we can be tempted to regard our understanding of the Eucharist as absolute and ultimate; we can be tempted to assume what happens is what we think happens. We might even begin to fashion a liturgy or text to better express what we think happens or should happen. The Eucharist can become a theological proposal or thesis rather than a theological oblation. In a theological oblation, our understanding or knowledge of the Eucharist is not equated with what theologically happens. God is the primary agent of the Eucharist. Our theological posture is always one of offering. We are present to give so that we might receive.

While the Roman Canon has the most longevity as a fixed text, it does include a variable section. After the dialogue and before the Sanctus, the Roman tradition has a "preface" that changes according to the liturgical season or feast day. Such variability of text is even more pronounced in non-Roman Western Eucharistic prayer traditions that emerged in the early medieval period. These traditions are associated with geographical areas of the West: Gallican, Mozarabic, and Celtic. Their Eucharistic prayers include entire sections that vary according to the liturgical occasion. However, beginning in the eighth century there was a move toward uniformity, or the imposition of tradition. At the beginning of the ninth century, Charlemagne sought to unite his empire in a number of ways, including required use of a common liturgy. He requested the rite of Rome for this purpose, and a sacramentary, which is a collection of prayer texts used for the Eucharist, was sent from Rome to Paris. A problem arose when it was recognized that this sacramentary was not comparable to the local tradition. The Gallican rite was more varied and expansive than the Roman rite, which was known for its simplicity. Charlemagne and his advisors decided to use the sacramentary sent from Rome, but added a supplement that retained some of the customary liturgical materials of the Gallican tradition. This decision, and its subsequent implementation, is an example of the imposition of tradition. The goal of uniformity was never entirely achieved. In fact, ironically, the hybrid Gallican-Roman rite later became known as the Roman or Western rite: A hybrid of traditions became the tradition.

Over the centuries, the various traditions and families of Eucharistic prayers, merged generally from their geographical locations into an Eastern or Byzantine rite and a Western rite. The Byzantine rite used a small number of Eucharistic prayers traced back to the fourth century, while the Western rite used the Roman Canon. This general division did not stop changes to the liturgy. Monasticism, cultural and intellectual shifts, as well as the political and theological machinations of the church induced further changes. The Eucharistic tradition became both authoritative and unwieldy. The liturgical tradition and the sacramental theological tradition took parallel but separate trajectories. While scholastic Eucharistic theology was not alien to the liturgy, it was not constructed as a reflection upon it. The relationship between the Eucharistic liturgical tradition and theological tradition reached a crisis in the Reformation, when the liturgy became the object of a strong and unrelenting theological critique.

TRADITION AS PROBLEM

The Reformers were united in their belief that the Roman rite as they knew it had gone astray. In their minds, it had ceased to be an authentic liturgical enactment of orthodoxy. The traditional liturgy was a gospel problem. Masses said by a priest alone, people rarely communicating, the chalice no longer given to the laity, the use of Latin, payment for Masses for the dead, the silent recitation of the Canon, the paucity of preaching, to give some prime examples, were all considered instances of a tradition gone awry. The Reformers' evaluation of the tradition as problematic was rooted in two authorities: Scripture and the early church. The normative principal of *sola Scriptura* operated in the liturgical sphere as well as the doctrinal one. While their knowledge of the patristic liturgies does not match our own due to the discovery of many sources in the nineteenth and twentieth centuries, the Reformers still turned to these liturgies as an authoritative marker for determining how far the Roman Church had strayed from "authentic" tradition.

Concerning the details of the Eucharistic liturgies, the Reformers went their separate ways. Luther retained some elements of a Eucharistic prayer, while Zwingli and Calvin surrounded the institution narrative with various prayers meant to instruct the people in proper Eucharistic theology. What these three figures have in common is a focus on the institution narrative. Jesus' words at the Last Supper stand alone as both authoritative and self-interpreting texts. Yet, even while these Reformers developed liturgies that positioned the narrative as foundational, and exclusively so, they differed on what the memorial means theologically regarding Christ's presence. They anchored their Eucharistic liturgies in the same text, but they did so from different theological boats.

The Reformation was not only a period when the Bible was pitted against tradition, but also tradition was used to "reform" tradition. Appeal to the tradition of the patristic church was prominent, especially in the development of the Anglican Eucharistic liturgies. While there were major shifts of texts that comprised the Eucharistic prayers of the Anglican Books of Common Prayer of 1549, 1552, 1559, and 1662 AD, they all retained a strong semblance to the earlier tradition. The example of the patristic church made a more direct impact on the development of Eucharistic liturgies and prayers outside of the official books of the Church of England. The Scottish and Non-Juror liturgies in the seventeenth and eighteenth centuries consciously adapted material that was prominent in the fourth century *Liturgy of St. James* and the eighth book of the *Apostolic Constitutions*. While the early tradition, as known and interpreted, was employed to deconstruct the Roman rite into a more putative biblical liturgy, it also was a resource for renewing the tradition of Eucharistic liturgies. Tradition was not only a problem but a possibility, depending upon one's view of the process or nature of tradition, and one's appreciation of varied traditions.

TRADITION AS POSSIBILITY

Beginning in the nineteenth century, but reaching a zenith in the twentieth century, liturgical scholars "returned to the sources." Scholars and church authorities alike conducted an extensive and ecumenically expansive discovery of, and engagement with, the liturgical documents of the early and patristic church. We considered some of these documents above in the section on "early witnesses" and in the section "normative witnesses." The investigation of sources and developments of the Eucharistic traditions laid the foundation for the reform of rites across all liturgical churches except Eastern Orthodoxy. Much of this scholarly work was ecumenical in scope, and exercised through doctoral programs in liturgical studies and academies of researchers. A convergence took place in the creation of new Eucharistic liturgies and prayers. A striking resemblance emerged among the official liturgies of most of the Western churches. The study of tradition reshaped its contemporary expression.

Interestingly, the recent convergence did not lead to a more definitive uniformity. The plethora of new Eucharistic liturgies demonstrates many similarities in shape and style, while still maintaining distinctive ecclesial identities. Churches whose tradition was to have one Eucharistic prayer now had several. Likewise, one church could not only have several prayers, but the prayers could have different structures, e.g. West Syrian and Egyptian. Along with this plurality and flexibility, a theological sensibility emerged that avoided a definitive assignment of moments of consecration and opposed, rather than complementary, viewpoints. A serious and sustained engagement with tradition for its own sake, and not as a way to proof-text the status quo, led to a renewed plurality and multidimensional appreciation of the nature and purpose of Eucharistic celebration, one that could be recognized across the battle lines of the Reformation. However, the shift from tradition as problem to tradition as possibility faces two countervailing forces: traditionalist tradition and deconstructed tradition.

TRADITIONAL CHANGE OR CHANGING THE TRADITION

Taking the tradition seriously, engaging it honestly, will yield change. We will discover that what we took to be ancient is in fact modern, what we regarded as primitive is innovative, while some other cherished ritual in fact has a dubious theological heritage. Yet, what we can gain from the habitual and disciplined engagement with, and really within, tradition is a sense of the vitality and self-correcting dynamics at work. Tradition is not something we can or should fix, but instead is a movement we learn to live into and out of; the way in which we are called to receive and hand on. However, if we are to be "traditioned" by the tradition, we must avoid two current forces or perspectives that each lack one pole of the movement of tradition: receiving without handing on, and handing on without receiving.

The traditionalist approach to tradition is a resistance to change; it takes one previous liturgical change as definitive. The traditionalist receives tradition without handing it on, without exerting any effort to place the tradition in hands that are not his or her own. We can try to hold on to what we suppose is the tradition, or try to remain in the place within the tradition that we like or in which we feel at home. We can make tradition our home but no one else's. The positive impulse to this approach is fidelity to what has been handed on to us. However, we should not equate fidelity with protection; we do not guard tradition. The past has given us a certain present, and it makes a present possible when it is allowed to speak with its own voice and not ours. Yet, the past speaks to us but does not dictate to us. Instead of freezing the present in a version of sixteenth or nineteenth-century Eucharistic liturgy, we can try to imitate our reconstructed version of a fourth-century liturgy. The past does not only serve as an apologetic for the status quo; part of the past becomes the model for radically altering the current state of Eucharistic celebration. We can find ourselves in a situation where we pit tradition against tradition. This is the abiding temptation to choose our own reality.

This same temptation can also be exercised in a completely different way. We can regard tradition as endemic to what is right, appropriate, needed, or desired. In order to hand on what is required now, we have to judge what can and cannot be received. Tradition can be an obstacle instead of a path to what the Eucharist "is really about." Tradition becomes more resource than source, and this development is aided by a move away from the one authoritative book of texts to a variety of (digitally available) texts from which to create a liturgy. The heightened capacity to put the pieces together ourselves deconstructs the liturgical tradition to an array of choices rather than as a formative whole. While in the past, uniformity was the Eucharistic agenda and proximate reality for many churches, now we observe the widespread desire for multiple liturgies reflecting different cultures, theological opinions, social values, and desired ends. A fair perspective would not extract these dynamics from or minimize their possible importance in any period of the tradition. But today's versions can operate with fewer limitations than hitherto due to the loss of the presumed authority of being "handed-on."

Change is intrinsic to the Christian life. Likewise, the Christian life has a tradition of living. As we experience change, and plan for change, we need to reflect first on how we are being changed and called to change logically and chronologically before we ponder what change we can enact. Liturgical change issues from those who are moved along through tradition, from those who have been formed traditionally. Traditional change occurs by the humble handing on of what we have received gratefully. Changing the tradition happens when it is objectified by an alien subjectivity. The celebration of the Eucharist is itself a receiving and handing on; it is the dwelling in the ritual place where things and persons are received without we having to create or produce them. These persons and things, and the structures and dynamics that present them to us, are gifts that turn their recipients into givers. Receivers become those who hand on; gifts are placed in our hands and we are to place them in the hands of others. The Eucharistic tradition is marked by a great throng of hands gathered over the expanse of all temporal ages; we should not lose sight of this, nor of the fact that some of those hands are ours and there are hands waiting to receive from us.

CHAPTER 2

PRESENCE

And remember, I am with you always, to the end of the age.

Matthew 28:20b

Is there a real presence of Christ in the Eucharist? For long stretches of the history of Eucharistic theology, this has been the dominant question. It is a question that has been debated for centuries and has received nuanced and negotiated answers in ecumenical dialogues on the Eucharist. Theologians and churches have been divided by this question: some answering yes, some answering no. In the course of these debates, each term has received its own scrutiny and understanding: real, presence, Christ, and Eucharist. One or more of these terms has shaped and can shape the debate in various directions. For example, a working sense of "real presence" arrived at apart from the other terms can lead either to a yes or no answer. If that is what we mean by real presence, how something or someone is really present, then we might say Christ is present that way or he is not. An array of philosophical strategies has been employed in the articulation and formation of what real presence is and is not. At times, theologians and churches have agreed on the premise that there is a real presence of Christ in the Eucharist but have disagreed on the nature of that presence and our understanding of it. Doctrines of real presence might be more affirmation than explanation or vice versa. We can affirm a real presence even though we cannot explain it, or we can explain it, which leads to an affirmation. Each term of the question implicates the others. Our understanding of the person of Christ may or may not allow for the declaration of his real presence in the Eucharist. An abiding argumentative appeal on different sides of the question has been the relationship between the divine and human natures of Christ. Christ is present in the Eucharist the way the human and divine natures present each other in the one person of Christ. Here, the incarnation becomes a focal point of the discussion. Yet, this discussion has been narrowly pursued by the concern whether, or how, Christ's body and blood are present with, through, or in the bread and wine. Is Christ really present to or in the bread and wine such that they become his body and blood? And if they do become his body and blood, what is the relationship between his "sacramental" and his "physical" body and blood? Our comprehension of one can negate the presence of the other. Our Christology can dictate our Eucharistic theology.

Where one goes with the question of Christ's presence in the Eucharist is not just the enterprise of ideas. The reality of Christ's presence or absence in the Eucharist does not take place in our heads. In fact, the Eucharist itself is not a mental exercise or construct. There are prayers and performances, texts and actions. What are we saying about Christ's presence in our prayers? What hopes are envisioned in our texts? Do we act as if there is a certain kind of presence of Christ available to us in the Eucharist? The actions of the ordained ministers, and of the congregation, articulate theological understandings, whether they are acknowledged or not. The development of Eucharistic theology was accompanied by changes in the celebration of the Eucharist as well as by shifts in piety. In the Reformation, liturgical texts and actions were created to express and support a particular theology of presence while disallowing other theologies or doctrines.

While the opening question is an abiding and critical one for Eucharistic theology, it is not altogether appropriate. Other questions and other avenues of inquiry are normative. Does the Eucharistic event as memorial fidelity to Jesus entail his presence? Is there a relationship between keeping memory and presence? Why do we celebrate the Eucharist? What do we say and do that speaks of Christ's presence? What is the nature and purpose of *Christ's* presence? These are the questions that emerge from the Eucharistic gaze; not questions put to the Eucharist but Eucharistic questions. Real presence of Christ means that the real Christ is present for Eucharistic reasons in a Eucharistic manner for a Eucharistic purpose. Reason is taken in two senses: why something is the way it is and how; and the adhering rationality of its purpose. Instead of pursuing an extrapolation of the incarnation into Eucharistic discourse, the presence of Christ should be explored paradigmatically in terms of the resurrection, ascension, and second coming. Christ as the incarnated person is present now as the risen, ascended, and promised one. The Eucharistic presence of Christ is first and foremost a new type of presence—a presence that can inhabit other types, while not being defined by them. When it comes to the presence of Christ in the Eucharist, we are not to seek the living among the dead. The promise of Christ's presence is not tethered to the history of human understanding or a product of human logical progression.

RISEN PRESENCE

Prior to turning directly to the question of Christ's presence *in* the Eucharist, and Christ's presence *as* Eucharist, I want to explore the nature of Christ's risen presence upon which any notion of real presence is contingent. This exploration will proceed by reflecting on two appearances of the risen Jesus. The first appearance considered is recorded in the Gospel of John:

> When it was evening on that day, the first day of the week, and the doors of the house where the disciples had met were locked for fear of the Jews, Jesus came and stood among them and said, "Peace be with you." After he said this, he showed them his hands and his side. Then the disciples rejoiced when they saw the Lord (John 20:19–20)

Jesus appears to the disciples behind locked doors. The conventional way of being in the presence of the disciples would be to announce one's intention of entering the room, and then be permitted to enter by those who had locked the doors. Without the will and action of others, Jesus would not be present. This is the way presence happens in the space and time shaped by the needs of fear and protection. All the more astonishing that Jesus appears without the will, action, or prior knowledge of the disciples. He is present in such a way that forces a re-definition, really a re-imagination, of what presence is and its possibilities. What confines us does not confine him. His presence is unexpected and unique; there has never been this kind of presence before.

The presence of Jesus is intentional: "Jesus came and stood among them." He went to his disciples to be with them; they did not just happen to be in the same place at the same time. Jesus' presence is the desire to be with his friends; it is an active presence. He speaks to them his word of peace amid their fear. He proclaims a reality contrary to their existence. The presence of Jesus is a word that is free of the context of its utterance. He does not question them about their experience; he does not seek to express the "feeling in the room." Instead, he brings a new word, free of the experiential contingency of its hearers. Though unique and free, this presence of Jesus is not without history: "He showed them his hands and his side." He shows them his history, the history recognizable to them, because, in a sense, they share this history with him. While his risen presence is not defined by previous parameters of presence, this presence bears the marks of history. The risen presence of Jesus can have a location without being localized in any known or expected way. He is present where he intends to be. He can speak the presence of a reality that was absent prior to his arrival. Yet, this free and noncontingent presence is still historical. The history of Jesus is present and available for our recognition, as a witness to what has happened to him in history without being the place where we find him: "Why do you look for the living among the dead? He is not here, but has risen" (Luke 24:5b).

Christ's Eucharistic presence will be intentional, locally undefined, noncontingent, and historical. Christ comes among the Eucharistic assembly in ways that do not comply with conventional presence. His Eucharistic presence transcends the conceptual boundaries we draw between presence and absence. Christ enters our celebrations of the Eucharist rather than being conjured up by and through them. This arrival is not contingent upon the emotional and intellectual state of the assembly. Christ is present to express his desire for us and not as a cipher for what we perceive to be our needs each time with gather. The history of Christ is present to us; indentifying him as the one who is present and not another. There is a particularity to this presence; while it may be available always and everywhere, it remains identifiable and primary. The history that is the presence of Christ is determinative for what is available to us in the Eucharist. No other history can take its place within the celebration of the Eucharist.

The most Eucharistically accessible account of an appearance of the risen Jesus is the encounter on the road to Emmaeus (Luke 24:13–32). Reflecting on this account can illuminate further our appreciation of the nature of the presence of the risen Jesus and its relationship to an appropriate understanding of Christ's presence in the Eucharist. I will divide the account into segments, considering each movement of the encounter for what it conveys about apprehending the presence of Jesus, and then conclude with some thoughts regarding Eucharistic presence.

> Now on that day two of them were going to a village called Emmaus, about seven miles from Jerusalem, and talking with each other about all these things that had happened.

These two persons were having a conversation about the recent events surrounding Jesus. This topic was uppermost in their minds, something pressing in on them, one of those topics that cannot be avoided. They cared enough about what had happened to talk about it, to make Jesus, and all that goes with him, the subject of their time and language. They were having a conversation about Jesus.

> While they were talking and discussing, Jesus himself came near and went with them, but their eyes were kept from recognizing him.

As they are talking about Jesus, he comes to them and travels with them. The subject of their conversation becomes present to them. And yet, even though Jesus is present, they do not recognize him. Here is a paradox of human discourse. When we talk about something, the subject of our attention has a presence. But we may not recognize this presence, because we are too absorbed in our language and thoughts. Our discussions can both reveal and hide what we are talking about. Maybe, we think our language for things or persons is sufficient for their presence, and yet we can be blinded to what this presence means and brings to our discussions and to our lives. They were talking about Jesus, and they could not recognize him.

> And he said to them, 'What are you discussing with each other, while you walk along?' They stood still, looking sad. Then one of them, whose name was Cleopas, answered him, "Are you the only stranger in Jerusalem who does not know the things that have taken place in these days?" He asked them, "What things?"

The subject of their conversation, the one who remains unrecognized, begins to question them about himself. They have been talking about Jesus but not with him, and Jesus breaks into their discourse with a question. The one about whom they are concerned inquires of them what they know. Jesus gets closer to them, nearer to recognition, by asking questions. They tell him the story, and how it had affected them. They know the story, they know what has happened, but they still do not recognize Jesus. Telling the story of Jesus is not the same as seeing him, as knowing you are in his presence.

> Then he said to them, "Oh, how foolish you are, and how slow of heart to believe all that the prophets declared! Was it not necessary that the Messiah should suffer these things and then enter into his glory?" Then beginning with Moses and all the prophets, he interpreted to them the things about himself in all the scriptures.

After hearing their recounting of the story, Jesus admonishes their ignorance and then tells them what it all means. Jesus teaches them the meaning of Scripture. The subject of Scripture is its interpreter. Even with this definitive interpretation of the events of the story in light of Scripture, Jesus remains unrecognized. Now they know what it all means, and still they do not truly see him. Knowledge does not necessarily lead to perception.

> As they came near the village to which they were going, he walked ahead as if he were going on. But they urged him strongly, saying, "Stay with us, because it is almost evening and the day is now nearly over." So he went in to stay with them.

They may not have recognized Jesus for who he really is, but they desire his presence with them to continue. They want him to stay with them through the end of the day. Perhaps, they might learn more from him about Scripture and this Jesus of Nazareth. For this to happen, they need him to remain on their journey. Note that they did not ask to go with Jesus where he was going. Instead, they asked him to be with them where they were going. Jesus is still part of their journey, and they are not part of his: Jesus remains unrecognized.

> When he was at table with them, he took bread, blessed and broke it, and gave it to them. Then their eyes were opened, and they recognized him; and he vanished from their sight.

After traveling with them, asking questions, hearing their story, teaching them the meaning of Scripture, staying with them on their journey, the two on the road to Emmaeus had still not recognized Jesus. It was not until Jesus performed certain actions that he was seen. These actions allowed them to see the Risen Jesus. These actions are the context for the perception of Jesus, for knowing that he is alive among them. They see him within these actions, but when the actions cease, he is absent. The taking, blessing, breaking, and giving of bread is the way that Jesus is seen in his resurrection, the way he becomes recognizable. Maybe, he joined them on the road to Emmaeus, and interpreted the Scriptures to them concerning himself so that they could see him risen through these actions. The taking, blessing, breaking, and giving of bread, the sharing of a meal with them, is the purpose of this presence, the intention of his arrival. They recognized him in the meal because this meal is now where and how he is viewed; where he is seen and known.

> They said to each other, "Were not our hearts burning within us while he was talking to us on the road, while he was opening the scriptures to us?"

Having seen Jesus through his actions, they are able to reflect on their previous experience of him. They now know that he was with them on their journey and in his interpretation of Scripture. Jesus' presence in the meal allows them to perceive that he was with them before and in other ways. The presence of Jesus through these actions illuminates where and how they were in his company but did not know it. Reflecting on Jesus' presence revealed on the road to Emmaeus can draw us more deeply into his presence in the Eucharist.

How susceptible are we to the presence of others? Are we aware of others well enough to perceive their presence? What does it mean for someone to be present to, with, and for us? When someone is present there is more there than a physical proximity; there is the possibility for a relationship of some kind. Our conversations, what we talk about, shapes our awareness of those who would, or would not, be present among us. Do we have conversations about the Eucharist, and do we have Eucharistic conversations forged by our repeated engagement with the Eucharist? To what extent are our discussions, deliberations, and negotiations within ecclesial discourse abidingly accountable to what we have seen, heard, and done in our habitual enactment of the Eucharist? These are questions of formation into the awareness of Christ's presence in the Eucharist. Yet, we can move from Eucharistic conversations that lead to an awareness of Christ's presence to a self-referential web of language that becomes an obstacle to his presence, a conceptual stone placed at the door keeping him from roaming freely among our ideas and words. The presence of Christ in the Eucharist can be unrecognized, because we remain in our own sense of what this means or not. It is as if we know the subject so well we are deciding who and what the subject really is. Our familiarity with the history of the subject can create distance between ourselves and its presence. Our knowledge of the history of speculation, understanding, and controversy regarding Christ's presence in the Eucharist must bring us to an awareness that yields to the kenotic moment when Jesus comes near and begins to question us. His Eucharistic presence questions all our Eucharistic answers. The presence of Christ is the interpretative perspective on all possible and permissible Eucharistic meanings. His presence is the arrival of how all these actions and words make sense. He brings his own coherence with him. Christ is present *in* the Eucharist and *as* the Eucharist.

Is Jesus on our Eucharistic journey, or are we on his? Like the two on the road to Emmaus, we can become intrigued by Christ's presence; it seems to serve some purpose for us. He helps us to understand some things that have puzzled us, or he can illuminate our spiritual journey. We want him with us where we are going. He is a companion but not the destination. Christ is really present in the Eucharist as the one who stands before us. Christ's presence is not the product of a thought experiment; we do not approach him through an extension of ideas. There are paradigmatic actions that announce his arrival: take, bless, break, and give. This is why I have spoken of Christ's presence in the Eucharist and as the Eucharist. The full array of actions that constitute the enactment of the Eucharist, what makes this event recognizable as the Eucharist and not something else, are markers of his presence. Again, Jesus has a recognizable history and a history of recognition.

While the Eucharist is the paradigm for Christ's presence, it is not the exclusive place of this presence. The Eucharistic presence of Christ opens us to the realization that Christ was and is already present in the several modes or ways that correspond to, and resonate with, the Eucharist. Through the Eucharistic actions, the two companions were able to perceive a previously unrecognized presence.

Any theology of Christ's Eucharistic presence should be both focused and expansive: focused within the Eucharist on the risen presence of Christ; and expanded beyond the celebration of the Eucharist to other manifestations of presence now viewed from a Eucharistic awareness and sensitivity.

WORDS OF PRESENCE

Throughout the history of Eucharistic theology, the institution narrative has been the touchstone for affirmations, speculations, and argumentations regarding the nature of Christ's presence and absence in the Eucharist. Some theologians have interpreted the same words in very different ways, while others have based their arguments on different words within the institution narrative. The version of the narrative from Matthew provides the words that have been given two disparate emphases. They are: "Take, eat; this is by body" (26:26b) and "Drink from it, all of you; for this is my blood of the covenant" (26:27b–28a). Analysis of these words, when performed within the climate of theological controversy, has tended to isolate one or two words or phrases. A phrase is used for an already established argument, and the phrase or word is dislocated from the complete narrative and its setting as text and as action. This analytical dislocation also occurs for the institution narrative and its place within a given Eucharistic prayer and within the economy of the Eucharist as a whole. In this way, the narrative, or a word or phrase contained within it, becomes a proof-text for a perspective constructed elsewhere.

The basic emphases of the words of institution are identity and commandment. Identity is affirmed by the assertion "This is" either "body" or "blood," and "eat" and "drink" are the commands. The identification of the bread and wine with the body and blood of Christ has been stated and understood in several different ways depending upon the theological climate of a particular period of the tradition. The commandment of Jesus to eat and drink has been given as the point of departure for Eucharistic theology by theologians who do not wish to entertain a real presence of Christ associated with the bread and wine. Often, the question is raised as to what authentic fidelity to Jesus' intention entails. Did Jesus give us words that will turn bread and wine into his body and blood? If so, fidelity entails the proper administration of those words to effect the desired conversion and communion. Or, did he give a commandment to eat and drink the bread and wine as the way to remember him? Fidelity here would involve proper remembrance. These two forms of fidelity are not necessarily opposed to each other, but they have been pursued at times as if they were. They can be related to each other by contending that the purpose of Christ's presence is for the eating and drinking of his body and blood. However, if the eating and drinking is meant as a sign of faith in Christ, and not as an act of consumption, then a "real" presence of Christ is denied. Here we are faced with another critical distinction among theological approaches to the question of the presence of Christ. Are we talking about a presence realized within the celebration of the Eucharist, or a presence already realized outside of the Eucharist to which its celebration signifies? "Sign" or "signifies" suggests something that points to a reality it does not share or convey. Are we dealing with words that announce a presence, realize a presence, or point to a presence? Are the words of the institution narrative not really about presence after all? We will explore possible answers to these questions by returning to some of the early witnesses of the Eucharistic tradition.

We do not have to wait until the Middle Ages for a direct statement that the bread and wine become the body and blood of Christ, and why this is so. The same document that provides the first complete outline of the celebration of the Eucharist has this to say on the topic of Christ's presence:

> For we do not receive these things as common bread or common drink; but just as our Savior Jesus Christ, being incarnate by the word of God, took flesh and blood for our salvation, so too we have been taught that the food over which thanks have been given by a word of prayer which is from him, (the food) from which our flesh and blood are fed by transformation, is both the flesh and blood of that incarnate Jesus. (Justin Martyr, *First Apology*, 66.1)

An abiding rationale for why the bread and wine become the body (flesh) and blood of Christ is an appeal to the incarnation. By the Word of God, Jesus is flesh and blood, and by this word the bread and wine become his flesh and blood. The purpose of this becoming is salvation and transformation of our flesh and blood by his. There is a continuum of identification and transformation: from incarnation through Eucharistic prayer to consumption. Jesus takes on our flesh and blood in order to transform it in the Eucharist. Justin relays that this affirmation of Eucharistic presence rooted in the incarnation is something taught. In the second century, if not before, there is a teaching of "real presence."

The *Apostolic Tradition* of Hippolytus is another early document containing teaching on the relationship of the bread and wine to the body and blood of Christ. Within his description of the Eucharistic prayer at the celebration of baptism, Hippolytus writes:

> And the offering shall be brought up by deacons to the bishop: and he shall give thanks over the bread for the representation, which the Greeks call "antitype," of the body of Christ; and after the cup mixed with wine for the antitype, which the Greeks call "likeness," of the blood which was shed for all who believed in him. (Ch. 22)

Here, we do not have a direct identification but a relationship of representation explained by use of a philosophical category. Such adaptation of philosophical language and categories to theological purposes is another enduring theme of a theology of Eucharistic presence. Theologians employ whatever is the customary way to think of reality, especially the relationship between the visible and the invisible. In this case, Hippolytus is utilizing the Platonic relationship between type and antitype. Type is the real, while antitype represents the type and participates in its reality. The type is accessible through the antitype without separation and complete identification. The physical body and blood of Christ is the type and bread and wine become the antitype through the prayer of thanksgiving.

As philosophical categories change, and the corresponding views of what constitutes the real and the true change, the language used and adapted for articulating the presence of Christ associated with the bread and wine changes as well. The intertwining of philosophy and theology can be such that theology changes along with philosophy. Also, what makes sense in one age may not make sense in another. What was assumed to be an affirmation of real presence at one time can be portrayed later as a denial of that presence. In this regard, the great shift in the adaptation of philosophy for theological purposes is from Platonic to Aristotelian understandings of the relationship between the visible and the invisible.[1]

In very broad strokes, the Platonic worldview is that there is an invisible realm-reality that is manifested in the visible. This relationship of sharing the real allows for the identification of the visible with the invisible without collapsing their identities into each other or without keeping them unrelated. As this view is developed, it yields an ontology of participation. The being or essence of one thing participates in the being or essence of another so that we cannot speak of the reality of one without speaking of the reality of the other. In the Eucharist, the bread and wine participate in the reality of the body and blood of Christ. With this philosophical background, the Patristic theologians could affirm the presence of Christ without seeking speculative clarity. The basic ethos of an ontology of participation qualifies anything said of the visible by the reigning mystery of the invisible.

Adapted to theological purposes by medieval theology of Eucharistic presence, the Aristotelian understanding of the relationship between the visible and the invisible is characterized by cause and effect: There is an invisible cause of a visible effect. Instead of the Platonic movement from the visible to the invisible, the Aristotelian movement is from the invisible to the visible. It is a movement that produces presence rather than a manifestation of presence. If presence is the effect caused by an action, then the question arises as to what is the appropriate action: What causal action produces this effect? Once the appropriate action is designated, then this action becomes regulated: You do this, and only this, to produce that and only that. The relationship between cause and effect becomes a linear and definitive one, which tends to exclude other possible relationships between the visible and the invisible within the realm of theology, especially any Eucharistic theology of presence.

The next development is a focus on the one who produces the effect and the one who speaks the definitive language of cause. The focus on the visible effect, while acknowledging theoretically that there is an invisible cause, can look for ways to usher in the cause within the ambit of the visible. A visible someone will have the responsibility for the productive action and its required accompanying language. The person will be said to have the power to produce the already defined effect. Taken this far, these developments, set in motion by the cause and effect view of reality, can lead to a loss of the inherent mystery surrounding any consideration of this world as not sufficient to itself. The loss of this metaphysical mystery can be compensated by practicing mystery, by practices deemed mysterious or thought to "produce" mystery. Certain practices within the definitive ritual can appear hidden and inaudible; perhaps, not all of the language is understood and is rationally available. The irony is that the loss of theoretical mystery becomes the gain of rituals of mysteriousness. Mystery is characterized by unknowing rather than by the inexhaustibility of knowing.

What I have been describing as the shift from Platonic to Aristotelian categories and movements between the visible and the invisible provides a very broad picture lacking nuance of Eucharistic theology and practice in the West. It reached a crisis in the Reformation.[2] The crisis was centuries in the making, combining both theology and practice as well as what people thought and did. Eucharistic theology of presence, while strongly affirming Christ's presence during the Patristic era, was never uniform. The same belief was expressed in a variety of ways and in different forms of explanation. The Patristic age of Eucharistic theology is characterized by different emphases without being directly shaped by controversy and argumentation. Certainly, this age was one of controversy and argument regarding the natures and person of Christ, the person of the Holy Spirit, and the Doctrine of the Holy Trinity. However, the literature on the Eucharist is more in the mode of reflecting upon its inherent mystery, its celebration, and what this means for the life of the Church and Christian living. The audience for this literature, whether sermons or catechesis, was Christians looking to learn and live the Eucharist more profoundly. What we do not have are theologians arguing with each other.

The standard treatment of the theology of presence in the Patristic period is exemplified in the works of Ambrose and Augustine and the distinction between their expositions of Christ's presence in the Eucharist. Addressing the relationship between the consecrated bread and wine and the body and blood of Christ, Ambrose emphasizes the real presence in the elements themselves. He upholds the notion that the bread and wine undergo a change. Augustine emphasizes that the bread and wine signify Christ's presence.

Ambrose is often assigned the role of the progenitor of the realist tradition of Eucharistic presence. Likewise, the progenitor of the spiritualist tradition is Augustine. He speaks of the elements as signs of the presence of Christ's body and blood that convey their reality. The sign is not extrinsic to the real in his use of the term. Rather, the sign shares in the reality of what it signifies due to their similarity or likeness. Augustine is working with the Platonic worldview. He does not speak of the change of elements such that they no longer remain bread and wine. Instead, he addresses the role of faith in receiving the body and blood of Christ. The presence of Christ is not solely the concern of what happens to the bread and wine, but what happens to the believer and to the church. This event of reception involves the faith of the receiver. While we can identify different emphases between Ambrose and Augustine, one realist and the other spiritualist, we can also find the concerns of each theologian in the work of the other. That is, there is realist language in Augustine and spiritualist language in Ambrose. The question is one of emphasis and not polarization. Augustine would say that Christ is really present in the Eucharist, and Ambrose would say that faith is essential to the economy of presence.

The markers of controversy appear in the ninth century and continue into the eleventh century. The *dramatis personae* in the ninth century are two monks from the same monastery: Radbertus and Ratramnus. In the eleventh century, they are Berengar and Lanfranc, a future Archbishop of Canterbury. Radbertus argued for the real presence through a change in the bread and wine; the true presence of Christ references his physical and historical body and blood. Ratramnus associated the elements with the body and blood of Christ through the use of the concept of "figure." This is a vestige of the Patristic language of "type" and "antitype" with its relationship of representation and similitude. However, now the conceptual ground had shifted, and employment of the terms of "figure," "type," "antitype," and even "sacrament" to express Christ's presence was suspect and thought to contravene the terms of "real" and "true." These lines of demarcation drawn in the ninth century continued into the eleventh century controversy. Berengar wrote in the tradition of Augustine and Ratramnus, and this got him into trouble with the church authorities. Lanfranc was the apologist for the more physical and historical sense of Christ's presence to which Berengar was deemed a threat. Berengar was forced to sign two oaths, the first using physical language to describe the nature of the presence of Christ's body and blood as the bread and wine. The first oath signed in 1059 AD is as follows:

> The bread and wine which are placed on the altar are after consecration not only a sacrament but also the real body and blood of our Lord Jesus Christ, and that with the senses not only by way of sacrament but in reality these are held and broken by the hands of the priest and are crushed by the teeth of the faithful.[3]

The elements became the physical, corporeal presence of Christ's body and blood. The "spiritualist" tradition of Augustine is eclipsed by a developing theology of presence in the key of the physical as opposed to the spiritual. No one, if pushed, would have thought that the body and blood of the historical Jesus ascended into heaven could be contained in a piece of bread and a sip of wine. Language can be marshaled as an opposing force to other language. The choice of words and ideas serves both to express what is affirmed and to negate what is denied; physical is not spiritual, visible is not invisible, temporal is not eternal, and locality is not universality. Why allow the visible realm to dictate terms to the invisible? Why should the "spiritual" be a theological threat to the "real"?

An irony of this narrative of how different emphases of presence become places to stand in opposition to each other, of how complementarity becomes argumentation, is that the actual celebration of the Eucharist in the West was reaching greater uniformity. Radbertus and Ratramnus knew the one Eucharist; they thought differently about the same event. Instead of generating theological creativity, the one liturgy somehow requires a corresponding authoritative intellectual clarity; doing one thing means one thing. However, while the textual tradition of the liturgy reached a basic singularity, various practices began to develop in the eleventh and twelfth centuries that begged theological questions. The liturgical celebration of the Eucharist can become standardized and uniform but it is never theologically neutral. One such practice was the elevation of the bread and cup at the time of the institution narrative. This action ritually demonstrated that the moment of consecration was the recitation of Christ's words, and the elevation itself engendered a piety of adoration. Even more so, when these words began to be accompanied by the ringing of bells and the censing of the elements, and the priest or bishop says them in a slow and deliberate way. Another practice that evolved was the replacement of leavened bread with the unleavened wafer. Cultural bread becomes cultic bread; only within the context of the Eucharistic celebration would the wafer be designated bread. Not only does the bread cease to have a resonance with common human living, it also loses its communal signification: each person gets his or her own wafer instead of a piece of a common loaf. Metaphors for bread give way to metaphysical musings on wafers, which are objects created for objective presence understood objectively. This is heightened by the hidden dimensions of the rite; the

Eucharistic prayer is said in an inaudible voice in a language (Latin) that does not belong to the people gathered. Added to this picture is the priest saying "secret prayers." The absence of liturgical transparency, coupled with philosophical anxieties about the visible, fostered a more focused and intentional effort toward theological precision.

In his argument against Berengar, Lanfranc used the word "substance." He introduced the distinction between the substance of something and its appearance. He sought a way to affirm that the bread and wine really and truly become the body and blood of Christ even though they still look and taste like food and drink. This distinction between substance and appearance receives its normative treatment in the thought of Thomas Aquinas. Considering the treatment of Aquinas, we would do well to keep in mind the possible disparity between the theologian himself and his later interpreters, as well as both official and pietistic versions of the doctrine of transubstantiation.

In the *Summa Theologiae* (IIIa, Q.75), Aquinas considers directly "the Change of Bread and Wine into the body and blood of Christ." Prior to delineating the relationship between truth and figure or sign, Aquinas confirms the role of faith in any apprehension of Christ's presence: "The presence of Christ's true body and blood in this sacrament cannot be detected by sense, nor understanding, but by faith alone, which rests on Divine authority." We take Jesus' word when he says "This is my body" and "This is my blood." We are to have faith in him that what he says is true. Faith approaches the invisible through the visible; we have faith in Jesus' divinity through his humanity. This is why, for Aquinas, there is a false dichotomy between a sign and the true or real. Christ's true body and blood are present as a sign. Aquinas also responds to the objection of real presence based on the argument that Christ's true body is in heaven and cannot be on the altar. He replies:

> Christ's body is not in this sacrament in the same way as a body is in a place, which by its dimensions is commensurate with the place; but in a special manner which is proper to this sacrament. Hence we say that Christ's body is upon many altars, not as in different places, but sacramentally: and thereby we do not understand that Christ is there only as in a sign; but that Christ's body is here after a fashion proper to this sacrament, as stated above. (art. 1)

Within the theological context of faith and the sacramental relationship between the visible and the invisible, Aquinas explicates how the consecration of the bread and wine entails a change in substance.

Aquinas argues that the substance of bread and wine is changed into the substance of the body and blood of Christ by means of the utterance of Christ's words: "This is my body" and "This is my blood." He makes this argument in contrast to another approach to the presence of Christ as one of substance. Usually referred to as "consubstantiation," this view holds that at the consecration of the elements, also through the form of the words of Christ, the substances of Christ's body and blood are joined to the substances of the bread and wine. Although he never uses the word "consubstantiation," Luther argued for this understanding of presence against transubstantiation on one hand and against the "sign only" view of Zwingli on the other. Luther invoked the doctrine of the incarnation's holding of the divine and human natures of Christ in one person as the ontological parallel to saying that the substances of bread and wine coexist with the substances of Christ's body and blood after the consecration.

According to Aquinas, endurance of the substances of bread and wine after consecration would negate the true presence of Christ. Quoting Ambrose to the effect that, while the figure of the bread and wine remain after consecration, only the body and blood of Christ are present, he precedes to analyze how one thing can become present in a place. Aquinas points out that for something to be in a new place, it either has to move there or be made anew by taking the place of something else. If something moves to a new place, it vacates an old place. We cannot say that the body of Christ is present through movement of place, because this body is in heaven and remains so. Rather, Christ's body and blood are present by taking the place of the substances bread and wine.

> And consequently it remains that Christ's body cannot begin to be anew in this sacrament except by change of the substance of bread into itself. But what is changed into another thing, no longer remains after such change. Hence the conclusion is that, saving the truth of this sacrament, the substance of the bread cannot remain after the consecration. (art. 2)

Turning once again to the words of Christ, the form of the sacrament, Aquinas posits that it is contradictory to declare "This is my body" and still think that the substance of bread remains, because bread cannot be said to be Christ's body. In this case, one would state "Here is my body." The substances of the bread and wine are not replaced or destroyed; they are converted or changed into the substance of the body and blood of Christ. What remains in the visible order are the "accidents," the outward and empirical appearances. Aquinas is adapting Aristotle's understanding that something exists as substance and accidents. The substance is what something is, while the accidents are how this something appears to us. For Aristotle, the accidents adhere in the substance, and they cannot be separated from each other. Aquinas uses this relationship to speak of Christ's real presence; he uses philosophy for a theological purpose and not a philosophical one.

We have seen that certain words of the institution narrative became the focus for the way the presence of Christ is to be affirmed and explained. The consecratory moment is Christ speaking the words "This is" to bread and wine whereby they become his body and blood. This identification between the elements and body and blood can be rendered in various ontological constructs. However, it was noted above that the institution narrative as words of presence receive two distinct, but complimentary, emphases. Besides a theology of presence focused on "This is," there is another theological perspective on presence that takes "eat" and "drink" as its point of departure. A liturgical example of this perspective is the Eucharistic prayer of the second Anglican prayer book of 1552 AD. The Eucharistic prayer of the first prayer book of 1549 AD was comparable in length and structure to the great prayers of the fourth century, even incorporating some parallels to the Roman Canon. Yet, this first prayer was an interim revision, and the full reformed project is exhibited in the second prayer. Lest there be any hint that a real and enduring presence of Christ is confected with the bread and wine eliciting pious acts of adoration, the prayer ends abruptly with the institution narrative and is followed immediately by the act of communion. Jesus commanded us to eat and drink and this is what we will do. The act of communion is a sign of the believers' obedience to Christ's command.

Any adequate theology of Christ's presence in the Eucharist will entertain not only how Christ is present but why. The purpose of the presence shapes, either implicitly or explicitly, the exposition of the nature of that presence. The role the bread and wine play in Christ's Eucharistic presence is affected by regard for the object of this presence: object as the elements, as the people gathered, or as the purpose. Jean Calvin was someone who interweaved these dimensions of Christ's "objective" presence. He strove to inhabit a middle ground between an overidentification between the elements and body and blood (doctrine of transubstantiation and Luther) and a nonidentification that held the act of reception as a sign of faith only residing solely in the spiritual realm (Zwingli). In his discussion on the nature and purpose of Christ's Eucharistic presence, Calvin interprets the institutional words of "eat" and "drink" within the context of Jesus' bread of life discourse in the sixth chapter of John's Gospel. As "the bread of life," Jesus is directing us to be fed by his body and blood in the Eucharist for the nourishment of our souls. In his *Institutes of the Christian Religion*, Calvin writes:

> That Christ is the bread of life, by which believers are nourished to eternal salvation, there is no man, not entirely destitute of religion, who hesitates to acknowledge; but all are not equally agreed respecting the manner of partaking of him. For there are some who define in a word, that to eat the flesh of Christ, and to drink his blood, is no other than to believe in Christ himself. But I conceive that, in that remarkable discourse, in which Christ recommends us to feed upon his body, he intended to teach us something more striking and sublime; namely, that we are quickened by a real participation of him, which he designates by the terms *eating* and *drinking*, that no person might suppose the life which we receive from him to consist in simple knowledge. For as it is not *seeing*, but *eating* bread, that administers nourishment to the body, so it is necessary for the soul to have a true and complete participation of Christ, that by his power it may be quickened to spiritual life. (*Institutes*, Book IV, Ch.XVII.V)

Calvin is opposed to equating faith with eating and upholds faithful eating. That is, by faith we receive the body and blood of Christ. Faith is not just a sign that we have faith in Christ. The contrast here between Calvin (and in a different way Aquinas) and the view represented by Zwingli can be expressed this way: faith in the presence or the presence of faith.

We can detect a shift away from the generative theological question of what happens to the bread and wine to what happens to the believers. Calvin speaks often of "participation"; through reception of the bread and wine as the body and blood we participate in the life of Christ. This participation is a dynamic movement among God, Jesus, the elements, and believers, "So the flesh of Christ is like a rich and inexhaustible fountain, which receives the life flowing from the Divinity, and conveys it to us" (*Institutes*, Book IV, Ch. XVII. IX). The presence as divine movement strains the categories of type and antitype, figure and truth, and substance and accidents. The relationship between the visible and the invisible cannot be negotiated by strategies of analogy and similitude. Rather than attempting to connect two entities in the same place and time, presence is comprehended as a participatory movement, a sharing of life, a crisscrossing of history and the world. In order to further this reflection on presence as participation, we need to recall that we are speaking of the risen presence of Christ, and at this point, to invoke the Holy Spirit.

THE SPIRIT OF PRESENCE

In addition to the theological tradition that the bread and wine become the body and blood of Christ by recitation of his words at the Last Supper is the textual and theological tradition that this change occurs through the invocation of the Holy Spirit. We saw in our examination of fourth-century Eucharistic prayers, especially the West Syrian type, that there is a consecratory *epiclesis* in the supplication section: an invocation of the Holy Spirit over the elements to "make" them the body and blood. The liturgical tradition of Eastern Orthodoxy, comprised of some of these prayers, has focused theologically on the invocation of the Spirit as the agent of consecration. The Western focus by contrast has remained on the institution narrative. We should recall as well the invocation of the Spirit over the people (communion *epiclesis*) that often accompanies the one over the bread and wine. Some examples of these invocations are the following:

> send down, Master, your all-Holy Spirit himself upon us and upon these holy gifts set before you, that he may descend upon them...and make this bread the holy body of Christ, (People: Amen) and this cup the precious blood of Christ. (People: Amen.) *The Liturgy of St. James*[4]
> send down your Holy Spirit on us an on these gifts set forth; and make this bread the precious body of your Christ, [changing

it by your Holy Spirit,] Amen; and that which is in this cup the precious blood of your Christ, changing it by your Holy Spirit, Amen. *The Liturgy of St. John Chrysostom*[5]

This pattern of invoking the Holy Spirit over the people and the elements is found in several other patristic anaphoras, which have served as models for the creation of many contemporary Eucharistic prayers. A distinction in the way Christ becomes present, or the way that the bread and wine are consecrated, has implications for a distinction in the nature of his presence. That is, on a theoretical basis, we are not necessarily talking about two ways to attain the same result. Different modes of becoming present can yield different types of presence. Again, we will explore this difference theoretically because we are not deciding how Christ is present, and what kind of presence he has. Reflecting on consecration through invocation will facilitate a more robust epistemological and ontological humility.

In the Western theological tradition, it has been customary to refer to the institution narrative as the "formula of consecration." The speaking of the words by the priest or the bishop within the context of the Eucharistic prayer produces Christ's presence; these persons are given the "power" to consecrate. There is a linear economy of consecration that is recognizable in the visible realm: a visible person speaks the visible words so that the invisible is present in a visible form. While acknowledging the primacy of divine agency, this economy can easily become circumscribed by the perceptions and expectations of human agency. Our theological sensibility can abandon contemplation for the sake of speculation; we can reach beyond affirmation to explanation.

When considering the presence of Christ in the Eucharist through the invocation of the Holy Spirit, and not the repetition of the dominical words, we are comparing the language of supplication to repetitive declarative language. The declarative words "This is" can render a fixed designation of something, an object that can engender a fixed account of its nature and presence. The language of supplication does not permit a linear economy of presence: when you ask for something to happen, you lose control over the result. Humans no longer speak the declarative words. Instead, we ask God, the divine agent, to act in a divine way for the sake of a divine presence. We place ourselves before the arena of divine action instead of inhabiting the place of divine action. We do not attain the presence of

Christ by speaking his words in his place. We do not even ask Christ to be present. The consecratory *epiclesis* is addressed to God the Father, and the Father is *asked* to send the Holy Spirit to make the Son present. This is a Trinitarian economy of presence that breaks the bond of any one-to-one theological configuration of presence, e.g. bread to body and wine to blood. The Trinitarian economy is a movement of mutuality so that identity is realized through identification "with" someone or something rather than creation of a separate entity that looks back at its creator by analogy or similitude. The Eucharistic posture is one of praise, thanksgiving, and supplication: praise for God as God, thanksgiving for what God has done, and asking that God act now. Christ is present to us and to the bread and wine through the sending of the Spirit because it is Christ's nature to be present pneumatologically, whether as incarnated, resurrected, or as Eucharist. This does not mean that Christ's presence is merely "spiritual."

Within the spectrum of possibilities, the Holy Spirit takes us beyond history and nature. When we entertain whether something is possible, whether it can happen or be the case, we look in two directions, toward nature and toward history. Nature constitutes our given capacities to be or become. Development or change in this regard is the outgrowth of what is already present; something or someone undergoes an extension of the self. When we raise the question of change, we ask if it is its nature to change, or is this possible change a natural one? Whether there ever has been this change is a question we pose to history. We look to history for patterns and evidence of change; it happened before so it can happen now. Unlike nature and its logic of inherent capacities, history is the story of the will, the landscape of human and divine action. We ask whether we can make something happen: can it possibly be done.

The invocation of the Holy Spirit is the petition to no longer be bound by the natural or the historical. However, this invocation is not the abandoning of nature or history. The Holy Spirit acts on nature, and there is a history of its action. Let us look at the place of the communion and consecratory *epicleses* in the economy of the Eucharistic prayer. Prior to the invocation of the Spirit, praise is given to God and thanksgiving is expressed for what God has done in history culminating in Jesus Christ. Some of the Eucharistic prayers emerging in the fourth century include creedal language of the Holy Spirit as "the Lord and giver of life." The invocation of the Spirit is preceded by a rehearsal of the act of the Spirit in Jesus' baptism and on the disciples at the day of Pentecost. These prayers recall God making history by redemptive acts and the role of the Spirit in bringing this redemption to fulfillment in the person and work of Jesus Christ. Thanksgiving for God's history and the remembrance of Jesus brings us to the moment of invocation, to the time when history will be made and remembrance will become presence. The economy of these Eucharistic prayers, and the place of the *epiclesis* within it, mirrors the economy of the resurrection.

In order to have an appropriate appreciation for the kind of presence involved in speaking of Christ's presence in the Eucharist, we reflected on two appearances of the risen Christ. Christ is present in the Eucharist, and anywhere else, as a resurrected person and body. Jesus did not raise himself from the dead; he was raised from the dead by the Father in the power of the Holy Spirit. Jesus' body was acted upon from outside his human nature and beyond his human history. The resurrection of Jesus is an act that is both continuous and discontinuous with his nature and history. Something happened that is not according to nature and yet continues the presence of nature. Something happened that has never happened before and yet continues the presence of history. Jesus is still who he is, and he bears the mark of what has happened to him. Nature and history in the risen person of Jesus are presented to us as the possibility of what nature and history are within the direct scope of divine agency. The presence of Jesus arrives from the Trinitarian act of God. The movement of his presence is from the invisible to the visible whereby the visible becomes the gift of presence. Theologically, we do not have to pry open a place within the visible in order to make room for the invisible. That place will always be an empty tomb. Instead, we are to wait outside for an appearance that will become familiar once we adapt to its strangeness. A theology of Christ's presence in the Eucharist is only appropriate and adequate when it is one of invocation and of resurrection. Of course, when considering the risen presence of Christ's person and history we are confronted by his absence, by the ascension.

ASCENDED PRESENCE

One of great conundrums of Eucharistic theology is how to understand and affirm Christ's real presence in light of his ascension. How can we speak of the body and blood of Christ being present in the Eucharist when they are present in heaven? Some theologians and churches have articulated positive answers to the question, while others insist that the heavenly presence of Christ's body and his Eucharistic presence are mutually exclusive. We noted above that Aquinas referred to the local presence of Christ's body in heaven in his argument for the change of substance between body and bread and blood and wine. Christ is not moved from heaven but comes to a renewed presence under the accidents of bread and wine. Luther argued that Christ's body could be present both in heaven and in the Eucharist. He appealed to the patristic concept of *communicatio idiomatum* to make this argument. Because we can predicate the properties of one nature to the other in the person of Christ, there is communication between what belongs to the human nature and what belongs to the divine nature and vice versa. We can say that because Christ's divine nature can be everywhere, omnipresence is a property of divinity, his human nature can be omnipresent as well.

The Reformers' view (not shared by Luther) was that the ascension of Christ's body does not permit this presence on the altar. To do so would be to negate his human nature; a dilution of the ascension has consequences for the incarnation. A liturgical example of a straightforward rendition of this view is found in the Eucharistic rite of the Anglican *Book of Common Prayer* of 1552 AD. Known as the "Black Rubric" because it was printed in black ink instead of red, it addresses the practice of kneeling to receive communion, and wishes to make it clear that such kneeling does not imply any adoration of "real presence" of Christ in the bread and wine. Rather, kneeling is a sign of a "humble and grateful" acknowledgement of receiving the benefits of Christ. The text continues:

> Leste yet the same kneeling might be thought or taken otherwise, we dooe declare that it is not meant thereby, that any adoracion is done, or oughte to bee done, eyther unto the Sacramentall bread or wyne there bodily receyued, or unto anye reall and essencial presence there beeying of Christ's naturall fleshe and bloude. For as concernynge the Sacramentall bread and wyne, they remayne styll in theyr verye naturall substaunces, and therefore may not be adored, for that were Idolatrye to be abhorred of all faythfull Christians. And as concernynge the naturall body and blood of our sauviour Christ, they are in heauen and not here. For it is

against the trueth of Christes true natural bodye, to be in moe places then in one, at one tyme.

The statement comes after the liturgy whose Eucharistic prayer does not contain an *epiclesis* and ends with the institution narrative. The natural sphere of existence is holding sway over the possibility of presence. In the visible realm you have presence or absence, but not both. This is the case for a nonresurrected and non-*epicletic* view of Christ's presence, a view that does not refer to a risen body made present by an agent other than itself. An alternative perspective on the problem of the ascension is proffered by Calvin. He writes:

> Though it appears incredible for the flesh of Christ, from such an immense local distance, to reach us, so as to become our food, we should remember how much the secret power of the Holy Spirit transcends all our senses, and what folly it is to apply any measure of ours to his immensity. Let our faith receive, therefore, what our understanding is not able to comprehend, that the Spirit really unites things which are separated by local distance (*Institutes*, Book IV, Ch. XVII.X).

The Holy Spirit unites what would otherwise be separated: divine and human natures, the living and the dead, past and present, and places of presence.

One way to relate Christ's ascended presence to his Eucharistic presence is the distinction between full and whole. The full Christ is present in the Eucharist but not the whole Christ; there is an absence to his presence. Christ's identity and presence are not collapsed into each celebration of the Eucharist; he is always arriving. We cannot appreciate his presence without acknowledging his absence. There is always more to his presence than our boundaries of space, time, and reason. His presence confronts us with our own absence from him. This is the kind of absence that does not lead to despair but to desire, the type of absence that provokes an awareness of the multiplicity of presences beyond the expected and the familiar. Christ's location in heaven, his ascended presence, gives us a horizon of presence, a vista of possibility, which we would not have otherwise. Contemplation of Christ's absence nurtures an imaginative presence; there is a presence not our own to which we might be placed. The humanity of Christ ascended and located in heaven is not a boundary but a bond. Who we are and what we are have a place within the life of God. In the ascension, we are present to God in an intimate and enduring way, a way to which we are invited, a way and a place for which we can hope.

COMMUNION OF PRESENCE

Eucharistic theology has been afflicted by myopia, the exclusive focus on Christ's presence in the bread and wine being the prime example. We can reduce the theological question to one of particular presence rather than of universal presence, or one type and not a multidimensional presence. Christ is present to the whole world in some way; he is not only present within the Eucharist. What is the relationship between his universal and Eucharistic presence? Grappling with this question as well as the specific question of Eucharistic presence, one should engage the fullest reflection available on Christ himself. Christology is the theological framework for Eucharistic theology, and Christology is itself not a self-enclosed category. There is a theological mutuality, even contingency between Christology and the Trinity. Ultimately, no matter the avenue pursued, whether Christology, Eucharist, doctrine of God, or ecclesiology, we arrive at communion as the accountable and doxological reality of all Christian life and thought. We will not traverse this whole territory at this point, but we will attend to communion as the way to conclude this chapter on Christ's Eucharistic presence.

There are multiple dimensions to Christ's presence in the Eucharist so that we might more appropriately speak of Christ's presence *as* Eucharist. Christ is present in the gathering of the baptized constituted as the Body of Christ. Those gathered for the Eucharist have been baptized into the death and life of Christ; they belong to his Body and have received the gift of the Holy Spirit. In the ancient church, one was not permitted to attend the complete celebration of the Eucharist unless baptized. One is made a member of the Body of Christ in order to receive his Eucharistic body and blood. One is baptized into Christ's receptive presence, into his kenotic availability to the presence of another, which is the receptivity that makes communion possible. Christ is present in the proclaimed Word of God, in the reading of Scripture. As the Word, he is present through the Word. Scripture is the narrative whereby we make sense of Christ's presence. As on the road to Emmaeus, he accompanies Scripture and its interpretation. Christ is present as the High Priest in heaven who hears our intercessions. Christ is present in the prayers of the people, the priestly prayers of the baptized. Two modes of Christ's presence as the Eucharistic prayer are memorial and invocation. Keeping the memory of Jesus means his history is present to us; he is present as his history, which can become ours. Giving thanks for this history places it before us as the reality where we discover our identity and vocation. This memorial is not just a look backward; the past becomes the fertile ground for the birth of new life, for the resurrection realized in our midst. In the Eucharist, Christ also offers an *epicletic* presence. The Holy Spirit is invoked so that we might receive him, and be received into his life of communion, the life that is Spirit-led and Spirit-filled. Through the action of the Spirit, the bread and wine, and the gathered baptized, are raised into the body and blood of Christ. Christ's presence is realized, and we share his reality. We receive the presence of Christ as communion with him, and for communion with him, and for communion with each other in him as he is a person of communion.

Our theology of Christ's Eucharistic presence should be characterized by his presence of communion. We are not required to abide in our various theologies of presence whether they are transubstantiation, consubstantiation, signification, or instrumentalism. "This is" identity is in communion with "Eat" and "Drink" commandment. Our theology of presence will be a communion among different emphases that have been placed in heaven, in the bread and wine, and in believers.

Our theology of presence ordered toward the gift of communion will have four primary attributes. These attributes are best appreciated in contrast to four other possible ones. The four primary attributes will be: contemplative more than speculative; affirming more than explanatory; expectant more than discursive; and receptive more than perceptive. There is a role for speculation, explanation, discursiveness, and perception but within the ambience shaped by contemplation, affirmation, expectancy, and reception. These primary attributes are distinct from the secondary ones, because they reside within the passive voice rather than the active voice. Theology is what we receive, and how we receive it, more than it is something we do, or how we do it. Christ's presence is received and not created.

The Eucharist is a liturgical event of the church (taken here in its broadest sense) that connects the baptized to Jesus as their salvation.

By liturgical event, I wish to emphasize that the Eucharist is not any type of ecclesial event, i.e., it is not juridical, magisterial, pastoral, or pedagogical. It is an event of ordered worship directed toward God and not a self-referential exercise of a community. This God-ward stance is critical for all reflection on the various dimensions of the Eucharistic celebration. There is an abiding horizon of transcendence, that which lies beyond the event and toward which the people are drawn. But the Eucharist is also an enacted transcendence by particular people in a particular place in a particular way with particular language. I say particular and not specific because there is variety to these liturgical events throughout the church and throughout the liturgical tradition. Yet it is precisely these particular actions and linguistic patterns that allow us to recognize the Eucharist and commit to its enactment as Eucharist. The Eucharist connects the people gathered to Jesus as their salvation. The nature of this connection has been treated in several ways, many of them in contradiction to each other. However understood, this connection is characterized as saving. That is, in the Eucharist a change is occurring due to Jesus, wherever this change is principally located, and however it takes place.

The Eucharist is an event of the mutuality of presences; Jesus is present to and for the baptized and the baptized are present to and for Jesus. These movements of presence have an asymmetrical relation. The baptized have a protocol of presence, certain basic actions are ordered along with a narrative for the sake of Jesus' presence, which cannot be defined or comprehended by such protocol. We engage in recognizable behavior for the sake of one who cannot be recognized in our conventional ways. The Eucharist is not a portrait of Jesus, but a set of actions and dispositions that make a place for him to arrive in his risen freedom. A correspondence between his presence and ours is not available to us in any reliable way from static realities, both material and mental. There is a correspondence characterized by gift, fidelity of action, and expectation. The presence of Jesus is the truth of the Eucharist. All that constitutes the Eucharist corresponds to the presence of Jesus as active reception, hopeful oblation, and kenotic rationality.

The Eucharist is an action performed so that the agents might be receptive to an act that proceeds from an agent not defined by, nor limited to, the event itself. The celebrants enact the Eucharist in order to become receivers of an action that introduces a realm of freedom which they do not share. Fundamentally, the Eucharist is enacted by the baptized so that there might be a divine action on them. In this way, our Eucharistic actions are not ordered toward our accomplishment, production, persuasion, or expression. Cause and effect relationships cannot be traced or logically supposed. Instead of acting toward a linear consequence, Eucharistic actions are renditions of passivity. The ultimate Eucharistic act is the presence of Jesus actively received.

We approach the presence of Jesus in hopeful oblation or expectant sacrifice. The correspondence between the presence of Jesus and our presence is the offering of self. Correspondence of presence is a movement toward each other.

CHAPTER 3

SACRIFICE

For as often as you eat this bread and drink the cup, you proclaim the Lord's death until he comes.

1 Corinthians 11:26

For almost fifteen hundred years, the sacrificial nature of the Eucharist was not controversial. However, once this controversy ensued in the sixteenth century with the onset of the Reformation, it has stubbornly remained. Two broad liturgical and theological trajectories account for this development. Liturgically (which is not separated away from theology, but a distinct perspective), there was a movement in the West from plurality of forms to the singular use of the Roman Canon and its repetitive language of offering and victim. Theological commentary on and interpretation of the liturgy likewise moved from an array of language and images to a definitive account of what happens and how. The Eucharist became a sacrificial system with an authorized economy run by the ordained priesthood. The development of a Eucharistic system, with its attendant theological apologia, was a key dynamic in the *theological* crisis of the Reformation. The Reformers' assault on the sacrifice of the Mass was integral to the hallmarks of their theology: *sola fidei, sola scriptura,* and the exclusive saving agency of God in Christ. For them, the sacrifice of the Mass, both in theory and in practice, was an offensive human "work" opposed to "faith." It struck at the heart of the nature and economy of salvation, of Christ's redemptive work. The theological divide between "Catholics" and "Protestants" has been maintained and formulated on the question whether the Eucharist is a sacrifice or not.

In order to delineate and identify the critical and abiding issues, theological and liturgical, involved in the question of Eucharistic sacrifice or sacrificial Eucharist, we will compare two signature documents that address the controversy from opposite sides: the Council of Trent's decree on the "Doctrine of the Sacrifice of the Mass" (1562 AD) and the *Augsburg Confessions's* article "Of the Mass" (1530 AD). Even though it was written later, we will consider Trent's teaching first, because it seeks to articulate what was the doctrine of the sacrifice of the Mass prior to and after the Reformation. The first passage comes from chapter I, "On the Institution of the Most Holy Sacrifice of the Mass." After stating that Christ is the priest who replaces the Levitical priesthood, and who offered himself in his death on "the altar of the cross" for our redemption, the chapter continues:

> nevertheless, because that his priesthood was not to be extinguished by his death, in the last supper, on the night in which he was betrayed, that he might leave, to his own beloved spouse the Church, a visible sacrifice, such as the nature of man requires, whereby that bloody sacrifice, once to be accomplished on the cross, might be represented, and the memory thereof remain even unto the end of the world, and its salutary virtue be applied to the remission of those sins which we daily commit, declaring himself constituted a priest forever, according to the order of Melchisedech, he offered up to God the Father his own body and blood under the species of bread and wine; and, under the symbols of those same things, he delivered (his own body and blood) to be received by his apostles, whom he then constituted priests of the New Testament; and by those words, Do this in commemoration of me, he commanded them and their successors in the priesthood, to offer (them); even as the Catholic Church has always understood and taught.

At the Last Supper, Jesus performed three actions: offered his body and blood under the species of bread and wine; gave his body and blood "under the species" of bread and wine to the apostles; and made the apostles priests of the New Testament. The memorial injunction is interpreted as Jesus' command to priests of every age to offer this sacrifice. The sacrifice offered in the Mass is visible and represents the cross, thereby applying its saving efficacy to sins committed daily (baptism remits original sin). Christ's priesthood and sacrifice, both at the Last Supper and on the cross, are continued by the priesthood of the church. A linear continuum of events links Last Supper, cross, and Mass enacted by Christ and priests of the church. Trent teaches that the sacrifice of the Mass was the sacrifice foretold by Malachi (1.11).

The efficacy of the sacrifice of the Mass is further explicated in chapter II of the decree: "That the sacrifice of the Mass is propitiatory both for the living and the dead." The sacrifice of the Mass is propitiatory:

> For the Lord, appeased by the oblation thereof, and granting the grace of gift of penitence, forgives even heinous crimes and sins. For the victim is one and the same, the same now offering by the ministry of priests, who then offered himself on the cross, the manner alone of offering being different. The fruits indeed of which oblation, of that bloody one to wit, are received plentifully through the unbloody one; so far is this (latter) from derogating in any way from that (former oblation). Wherefore, not only for the sins, punishments, satisfactions, and other necessities of the faithful who are living, but for those who are departed in Christ, and who are not fully purified, is it rightly offered, agreeably to a tradition of the apostles.

The distinction made between Christ's offering on the cross and in the Mass is one of manner: one is bloody and the other is unbloody. The continuity of the two offerings allows for the Mass to be a propitiatory sacrifice: an event of the forgiveness of sins. This teaching involves a confluence of agencies between Christ and priests. Christ is the offerer and the victim offered; he offers himself in the Mass through the priest's action as he offered himself on the cross. The agency of offering is twofold: Christ and the priest. The agency of applying Christ's sacrifice belongs to the church and its priesthood. The sacrificial act of the priest for the living and for the dead is expressed in the prayers of the priest made just before reciting the Canon of the Mass. One of these prayers (*super oblata*) from the Missal of 1571 AD clearly articulates the priest's role:

> Receive, holy Father, almighty eternal God, this unblemished offering which I, your unworthy servant, offer to you, my living

and true God, for my innumerable sins, offences, and negligencies; for all who stand around, and for all faithful Christians, alive and dead; that it may avail for my salvation and theirs to eternal life.[1]

The liturgy and the teaching on the Mass are infused with the language of offering and sacrifice. The priest is the agent through whom Christ is present and offered. The theological economy of Christ's saving work, the cross, church, priesthood, and Mass exist in such a state of mutuality that it can be difficult to gain clarity of who does what and when. It is a complex fabric; pulling one thread would unravel the whole. Any alien perspective on one of its components, e.g., priesthood or cross, would threaten the theological integrity of the entire system. The Reformers' radical separation of faith and works, of divine and human agency, meant they could not leave the Mass, sacrifice, and priesthood unchanged, unreformed.

The article, "Of the Mass," in the Lutheran *Augsburg Confession* begins by dismissing the charge that the celebration of the Mass has been abolished. The Mass continued to be celebrated reverently and with sound teaching; what has been eliminated are Private Masses (when only the priest, or maybe with a server is present). These Masses are done predominately for money, and as a consequence, have been greatly multiplied. Compounding this abuse is the view that the cross of Christ remits original sin, while the sacrifice offered in the Mass remits the daily sins of the living and of the dead. The article then states:

> For Christ's passion was an oblation and satisfaction, nor for original guilt only, but also for all other sins, as it is written to Hebrews, 10,10: We are sanctified through the offering of Jesus Christ once for all. Also, 10,14: By one offering He hath perfected forever them that are sanctified. [It is an unheard-of innovation in the Church to teach that Christ by His death made satisfaction only for original sin and not likewise for all other sin. Accordingly it is hoped that everybody will understand that this error has not been reproved without due reason.]

Having addressed the teaching and practice of the Roman Church, the article proceeds to set the Mass within the context of justification by faith. This context determines what happens to the gathered believers.

Scripture also teaches that we are justified before God through faith in Christ, when we believe that our sins are forgiven for Christ's sake. Now if the Mass take away the sins of the living and the dead by the outward act justification comes of the work of Masses, and not of faith, which Scripture does not allow.

Christ's memorial command, "Do this in remembrance of me," is quoted and interpreted as an exhortation for those who receive the sacrament to "remember" what they receive from him. The Mass is when Christ offers his "benefits" to the faithful and not when they offer. The sacrament can "comfort the anxious conscience" and is given to those persons who "have need of consolation."

The teaching of Trent and the *Augsburg Confession* agree that the Mass is for sinners. However, for Trent, the sacrifice of the Mass is the act that remits sins, and for the *Confession*, the Mass comforts sinners by reassuring them that through faith they receive the saving effects of Christ's cross. Put another way: either sinners must offer sacrifice or sinners cannot offer sacrifice. Is the chasm between these two authorized teachings bridgeable? Do we have to choose between them or reject both as understandings of the relationship between the Eucharist and the cross?

LUTHER, THE MASS, AND HEBREWS

In order to begin to answer these questions, and to deepen and clarify our grasp of the different theologies of sacrifice presented thus far, we will explore two expositions of the Mass as a sacrifice: one by Luther and the other by the theologians at the Council of Trent. A guiding theme of their respective views is how they employ the Epistle to the Hebrews. This Epistle, with its images and language of sacrifice, priesthood, and the propitiation for sins, provided the grammar for argument. It was how they argued even though they were arguing against each other.

Before he began to write on the Mass, and whether or not it is a sacrifice or not, Luther lectured on the Epistle to the Hebrews at the University of Wittenberg in the summer and winter semesters of 1517–1518 AD. In these lectures, he expounded the interpretations of verses that he would bring to bear in his later writings on the Mass and sacrifice. We will consider the first of these writings and the use of Hebrews found in it.

Luther published his *Sermon on the New Testament, that is, the Holy Mass* (hereafter *Sermon*) in July 1520 AD. In this essay, he presents his understanding of the Mass as the testament of Christ. On this basis, he opposes the Roman Catholic theology and practice of the sacrifice of the Mass, and he expresses his approach to sacrifice and priesthood. Luther employs of an array of verses from the Epistle to the Hebrews in the course of his argument. He relies on Hebrews 9:16–17 as the starting point for his foundational claim that the Mass is Christ's testament and not a sacrifice. He appeals to Hebrews 13:15 to describe the kind of sacrifice that Christians can offer. Hebrews 9:24 provides the way for Luther to describe the priesthood of Christ as his heavenly intercession on behalf of Christians. Lastly, he refers to Hebrews 11:6 when emphasizing the necessity of faith for the reception of the sacraments.

Foundational to his understanding of the Mass is Luther's application of the category of testament to Christ's words at the Last Supper, especially the phrase, "This is the cup of the New Testament" (Luke 22:20). This phrase is interpreted with reference to Hebrews 9:16–17, which states that a testament is ratified at the death of the one who made it. For Luther, Christ's testament, established at the Last Supper and ratified by his death, is "new" because it abrogates the Old Testament. He reasons that the Old Testament was concerned with temporal things; it was given through Moses and promised the land of Canaan. God did not die in the Old Testament, but the slain paschal lamb prefigured the death of Christ. The New Testament is eternal and becomes effective at Christ's death, and it promises eternal things: the forgiveness of sins and eternal life. Also, as with every promise made by God, Christ's testament comes with an attached sign. This sign is the sacrament of Christ's body and blood in the form of bread and wine. In his *Lectures on Hebrews* (hereafter *Lectures*), Luther identifies Hebrews 9:17 with Christ's words over the cup. He delineates a correspondence between the traits of a civil testament and how they are found in Christ's institution of the Mass: it was established prior to death; it bequeathes the forgiveness of sins and eternal life; its heirs are those who have faith in Christ; its witnesses are the apostles and the Holy Spirit; and Christians are to respond to Christ's testament by fidelity to the injunction, "Do this in remembrance of me" (Luke 22:19; 1 Corinthians 11:24). This remembrance, according to Luther, is the Christian's proclamation of Christ's death, which accomplished the forgiveness of sins and eternal life for the heirs of the testament. In the *Sermon*, the components of Christ's testament are succinctly identified as follows: the testator is Christ; Christians are the heirs; the testament itself is Christ's words at the Last Supper; the sign is the sacrament of bread and wine; the blessing (or inheritance) is the forgiveness of sins and eternal life: and the duty of the heirs is to remember Christ by proclaiming what he has done for them. Because the Mass is Christ's testament, the Christian can only receive its benefits in faith. Luther contrasts faith as preparation for Mass with acts of penitence.

> Let someone else pray, fast, go to confession, prepare himself for the mass and the sacrament as he chooses. You do the same, but remember that this is all pure foolishness and self deception, if you do not set before you the words of the testament and arouse yourself to believe and desire them.[2]

Faith is the only way Christians are able to receive what God promises. As Christ's testament, the Mass is an event when Christians receive what has been done for them, which they cannot do for themselves. Faith is opposed to works; the Mass is a sacrament to be received in faith, not a work to be done.

While Luther argues in the *Sermon* that the Mass is a testament and cannot be a sacrifice, he does not eliminate any sacrifice or offering from taking place within it. Regarding the sacrifice of Christ on the cross and the sacrament of Christ's body and blood, the Mass cannot be a sacrifice or sacrificial. However, Luther turns to another sphere of Christ's action to speak of what Christians can offer in the Mass: Christ's heavenly priesthood. Christians can offer themselves and prayer in the Mass to Christ the priest interceding for them in heaven. He uses two verses of Hebrews to relate our sacrifice of praise and thanksgiving (13:15) to Christ's priesthood (9:24). After examining these verses, along with Psalm 110:4 and Romans 8:34, Luther summarizes how Christ's testament and priesthood allow for a sacrificial offering of Christians but disallows the Mass itself to be distinct sacrifice.

> From these words we learn that we do not offer Christ as a sacrifice, but that Christ offers us. And in this way it is permissible, yes, profitable, to call the mass a sacrifice; not on its own account, but because we offer ourselves as a sacrifice along with Christ. That is,

we lay ourselves on Christ by a firm faith in his testament and do not otherwise appear before God with our prayer, praise, and sacrifice except through Christ and his mediation. Nor do we doubt that Christ is our priest or minister in heaven before God. Such faith, truly, brings it to pass that Christ takes up our cause, presents us and our prayer and praise, and also offers himself for us in heaven.[3]

Christians do not offer Christ; they offer themselves to Christ. In faith, Christians receive the saving benefits of Christ with thanksgiving. The offering of Christians in the Mass is a response to Christ's offering for them. They do not attain salvation through their offering. Luther uses various verses of Hebrews to make a decisive distinction: The Mass is not a sacrifice but is still sacrificial.

TRIDENTINE THEOLOGIANS AND HEBREWS

How did theologians of the Roman Catholic Church respond to the Reformers' abrogation of the sacrifice of the Mass, and especially, how did they use Hebrews to do so? We will look at the debates and submissions of the theologians who gathered in Bologna in 1547 AD for the first session of the Council of Trent.[4] The schema of the debate was provided by seven articles that summarize the Reformers' theological and liturgical objections to the Mass as a sacrifice. Our foray into the thinking and arguments of the theologians will provide a view into the state of the question of Mass and sacrifice at a pivotal period for its understanding. However, we need to appreciate that the theology of the Mass presented below is in the mode of defense or apologetic. The theologians are countering opposing perspectives; they are interpreting Hebrews over against other interpretations.

The theologians' discussion of the first article provides an adequate picture of their understanding of the Mass as a sacrifice and how they sought to meet the objections of the Reformers and their use of Hebrews. The first article for debate states that the Mass is not a sacrifice and an offering for sin but a commemoration of the cross. Various themes emerged in the course of their deliberations of this article, and within their written submissions regarding it. These themes and the theologians' corresponding use of Hebrews are: the relationship between the cross and the Mass (verses that speak of the uniqueness of the cross); priesthood offering the Mass (5:1); old law in relationship with new law (7:12); and Melchizedek as a type of Christ (5:6 and chapter 7).

The primal question facing any deliberation of the sacrificial nature and purpose of the Mass is how does this relate to the once-for-all event of Christ's cross. Once there is *the* sacrifice, can there be any others? One way the theologians distinguish between cross and Mass is to say that the cross is a bloody sacrifice and the Mass is an unbloody one. Addressing the Reformers' use of the verses of Hebrews that uphold the once-for-all nature of the sacrifice of the cross, the theologian Antonius Riccius argues "it is true that Christ died once and was offered bloodily; but in the Mass Christ does not die nor suffer, but it is done in memory of this death. The same bloody sacrifice which was made on the cross, is unbloody in the Mass."[5] Another argument of some theologians was based on a distinction between the mortal and the immortal Christ. The mortal Christ was offered on the cross, and the impassible and immortal Christ is offered in the Mass. For Alexander de Lugo, Hebrews excludes another sacrifice that took place on the cross but not offerings of the immortal and invisible Christ who cannot suffer or die.[6]

Another strategy for responding to the Reformers' insistence on the singularity of the cross as articulated by Hebrews was to outline various ways in which Christ is offered. Alexander de Bononia posited two ways in which Christ is offered. The first way is the offering of Christ's body and blood under the species of flesh and blood; this is what happened on the cross and is the referent of Hebrews. The other way Christ is offered is under the species of bread and wine on the altar, and this offering signifies Christ's previous offering on the cross.[7] Another theologian who makes the double sacrifice argument in the face of the once-for-all verses of Hebrews (7:27 and 9:12,28) is Thomas de Sancto Marino. Sacrifice is twofold: the propitiatory sacrifice offered for the remission of sins, which reconciles us to God; and the sacrifice of praise and actions in service and honor to God. The first type is the subject of these verses of Hebrews, and the second type is dependent on the first as its cause. This second type is the Mass in which Christ's passion is commemorated, and because the Mass is a memorial of the cross, it too is a sacrifice. For Thomas de Sancto Marino, "Christ is sacrificed on the altar sacramentally and mystically, because in the sacrament of that [sacrifice on the cross] which was once made."[8] Both the theologians of Trent and Luther could acknowledge that the Mass is a sacrifice of praise rendered to

God, but what they could not agree on was whether the Mass is an offering for the remission of sins.

While the Reformers would agree that the Mass is done in memory of the cross, they would disagree over the nature of this memorial. The theologians at the Council of Trent repeatedly held that the Mass is a sacrifice because it is done in memory of Christ's sacrifice on the cross. A representative of this view is Iohannis Franciscus de Cesena. He reasons that because the sacrifice of the cross is propitiatory, as Hebrews 9:13 says, the Mass also is propitiatory because it is a memorial of the cross. The Mass is not only a memorial of the cross; it is an actual offering of Christ. The identity between Mass and cross is preserved due to their respective offerings of the same Christ. Cesena makes the customary distinction between the bloody offering on the cross and the unbloody offering made with the consecrated bread and wine.[9]

In was incumbent on some of the theologians to discuss the priesthood in connection with their apologetic for the sacrifice of the Mass, and in doing so they relied upon Hebrews 5:1: "Every high priest chosen among mortals is put in charge of things pertaining to God on their behalf, to offer gifts and sacrifices for sins." For the most part, Luther interpreted this verse to refer to Christ, while Tridentine theologians considered it a reference to the priesthood of the church. The existence of a priesthood described by this verse means that there is a sacrifice for them to offer: a sacrificial priesthood entails a sacrifice for sins. This logic is typically displayed by Antonius Riccius as follows:

And when Paul says, that it is proper for the priesthood to offer "gifts and sacrifices for sins," it follows, which it ought, in order that we might say, either that there would not be priests in the Christian church, if the Mass is not a sacrifice; or that the Mass would be a sacrifice, if there are priests in the Christian church since we have no other sacrifice and priests are not able to be without sacrifice.[10]

Other theologians linked the existence of the sacrificial priesthood with Jesus' command at the Last Supper, "Do this in remembrance of me."

The propriety of a sacrificial priesthood in the church, along with the supportive use of Hebrews 5:1, calls into question the relationship between the Old and New Testaments, the old law and the new. Is this relationship one primarily of continuity or discontinuity? Did Christ's sacrifice on the cross end all other sacrifices, or did it change the type of sacrifices offered? Claudius Zaius argued that every type of law has the mandate to offer sacrifice, and this is the case both for natural law and the law of Moses. This means that the law of the Gospel should likewise have priesthood and sacrifice even though it is different than the ones of the old law. As do other theologians making this argument, Zaius appeals to Hebrews 7:12, "For when there is a change in the priesthood, there is necessarily a change in the law as well." He states:

> And if priests should be in the law of the gospel, it is necessary that there also be sacrifices, as Paul said, for it is proper for them to offer. But there is no other sacrifice in the law of the gospel unless it is the oblation of the eucharist; therefore this oblation is a sacrifice.[11]

The thesis that there is a necessary continuity between the law, priesthood, and sacrifice of the old and new covenants, with the appeal to Hebrews 7:12, is put forth by several other theologians. However, the continuity between the two laws, covenants, or testaments is comparative: the new is 'more perfect' than the old.

Even though the theologians at Trent sought to establish a continuity of priesthood and sacrifice between the Old and New Testaments, they insisted that the church's priesthood and sacrifice are different. For a type of this difference, some of them appealed to the figure of Melchizedek. Responding to the Lutherans' conviction that there is no sacrifice in the new law, Alexander de Lugo turns to the "sacrifice" of Melchizedek, which prefigured in the old law what would be in the new law. Melchizedek's offering of bread and wine resembles more the sacrifice of the altar than the cross. On the cross, the priest and victim were the same, but in the Mass, the priest and victim or oblation are different as was the case for Melchizedek.[12] The argument that the sacrifice of the Mass was prefigured by the sacrifice of Melchizedek is bolstered by the identification of his priesthood with Christ's. According to Alphonsus Salmeron, Melchizedek is a figure of Christ (Hebrews 5:6), and this means that Christ too is an eternal priest (Psalm 110:4). Although Christ offered himself once to the Father (Hebrews 7:27; 9:28; and 10:14), Christ is still "a priest forever" (Hebrews 7:21,24). Salmeron's juxtaposition of the once-for-all sacrifice on the cross with Christ's eternal priesthood leads to the assertion that priests of the church continue the priesthood of Christ, prefigured by Melchizedek, by offering bread and wine on the altar in the name of Christ.[13]

We have been reviewing the theological divide between Lutherans and Roman Catholics regarding the sacrifice of the Mass. First, this division was articulated by official teaching arising in the course of the Reformation in the sixteenth century. Next, we explored the theology behind the teachings in an essay by Luther and in the submissions of theologians at the first session of the Council of Trent, focusing on their respective use of the Epistle to the Hebrews. We may well ask about now, in this age of ecumenical dialogue and agreements, is there still a theological divide between Lutherans and Roman Catholics regarding the nature and purpose of the Eucharist as a sacrifice?

The statement of the Eucharist by the Lutheran/Roman Catholic International Commission strives to express what is held in common and what still is not. When addressing what is common, in the section "Giving of self," it reads: "When the church actually follows the command of the Lord: 'Do this in remembrance of me!' (Luke 22:19; 1 Corinthians 11:24f), it comes into contact with the sacrifice of Christ anew; it receives new life from Him and the power to die with Him." The "contact" the Eucharist has with the cross is dynamic and saving. As do other ecumenical dialogues, "memory" is treated as an efficacious reality whereby the past shapes the present and not just as a psychological recalling. The movement is less one from a past event to a present mind and more a movement of believers to Christ and his offer of salvation:

> All those who celebrate the Eucharist in remembrance of Him are incorporated in Christ's life, passion, death and resurrection. They receive the fruit of Christ's offering his life and thereby of the entire reconciling saving act of God. (paragraph 36)

The relationship between the cross and the Eucharist allows for a sacrifice of praise to be offered liturgically. The sacrifice of Christ is the "content" of the sacrifice of praise; it is a joining of the believers to Christ and his priestly intercession before the Father.

While there is common ground for Lutherans and Roman Catholics to stand on, this does not mean that they do not still stand on different spots. After agreeing that Christ is present as crucified and risen, and that the cross is a once-for-all event that cannot be "repeated, nor replaced, nor complemented," the statement does say that Christ's sacrifice "should become effective ever anew." It then acknowledges that "there are different interpretations among us regarding the nature and extent of this effectiveness." (paragraph 56)

The statement rehearses and maintains the historic "different interpretations" that still abide. Trent's teaching that a propitiatory sacrifice is offered in the Mass is recalled. The offering that the believers make is joined with Christ's offering. They participate in this offering outwardly and inwardly; bread and wine are offered as preparation for Eucharist, and the inner self is aware of complete dependence upon God's power. The full participation of Christians in Christ's priesthood and sacrifice permits the understanding that an offering of Christ takes place in the Eucharist; there is a mutuality between Christ offering us and we offering him. The Catholic position will not let go of the act of "offering Christ," while it attaches the Reformed caveats that we do not merit salvation and can do nothing on our own without Christ and the working of the Holy Spirit.

From the Lutheran side, the concern to uphold the unique and sufficient character of Christ's sacrifice has meant a rejection of any concept of the Eucharist as a propitiatory sacrifice. Lutherans continue to deny the phrase "sacrifice of the Mass." What is at stake is that when it comes to Christ's saving work, Christians can only receive this in faith. There is only one salvific movement in the Eucharist: Christ to Christians and not vice versa. The sacrifice of thanksgiving that occurs in the celebration is a response to this saving movement; it is has no role in the economy of salvation.

ENDURING QUESTIONS

Thus far we have reviewed the main lines of controversy regarding the Eucharist as sacrifice that began in the sixteenth century. We traced the two fundamental sides of the debate represented by the Lutheran and Roman Catholic churches. Doctrinal statements issued at the initial stages of the controversy were examined, and our understanding of their positions were broadened and deepened by turning to the arguments of Luther and the theologians at the Council of Trent. Finally, we checked the contemporary state of the question by looking at the statement on Eucharistic sacrifice issued by the international Lutheran-Roman Catholic Commission. Two sets of concerns and two avenues of further deliberation are before us. One set is the identification and classification of the enduring questions surrounding the relationship between the Eucharist and Christ's sacrifice on the cross. The second set is the attempt to transcend the controversy by placing it within a broader, and more appropriate, theological context. This section of the chapter will take up the first set of concerns, while the next and final section will deal with the second set.

The fulcrum point of the debate and controversy, and hence of the abiding divide among Eucharistic churches, is the relationship between cross and Eucharist. Is there a relationship that permits us to regard the Eucharist as a sacrifice, to hold that a sacrifice or offering occurs within the Eucharist, or should we banish all possible notions of sacrifice from its celebration? The divide can be mapped along these three possible relationships, and it can be marked by the choice of prepositions used in its paradigmatic phrase. The Eucharist is a representation *of* the cross, an application *of* the saving effect of the cross, or a different manner (bloody/unbloody) *of* offering the same sacrifice. Another perspective would stress that the Eucharist is a participation *in* the saving event of the cross. A theological stance that strives to keep the cross and the Eucharist soteriologically distinct would say that the Eucharist is a response *to* the cross and Christ's saving work. There is a world of theological difference between the "of" and the "to" with the "in" as a possible bridge between them.

Is the Eucharist a sacrifice? The answer to this question begins with the recognition that the concept of "sacrifice" has a history of use and has multiple referents. Etymologically, sacrifice can mean to make something holy. In antiquity, both Hebrew and pagan, a sacrifice often involved killing an animal to appease a god or to retain or regain a positive relationship with a deity. In the prophets, the Hebrew concept of sacrifice was expanded to the lives of people: the sacrifice of the inner self and the living of sacrificial lives. God desires that we offer ourselves and not only a surrogate. The cross of Christ is interpreted as an offering on our behalf and as an offering we share with and in him. The cross and Christ's death is an event accomplished for us as well as a provocation to be sacrificial ourselves. The question is always a relational one; the nature of "between" keeps being drawn. What is the nature of the relationship between Christ's sacrifice and ours? Do we share in Christ's, do we apply it, represent it, repeat it, remember it, or respond to it? Do any of these relationships between Christians and Christ's sacrifice have any place within the Eucharist? Of course, this raises the normative questions for understanding of the Eucharist: why, what, and how.

From the cross side of the equation, there is a tendency to isolate the cross along with its attributed meaning: Christ died for the forgiveness of sins. When relating the cross to the Eucharist, or is relating Eucharist to cross, we can apply one definitive view of cross to another definitive view of Eucharist so that the two "fit" together. The problem with definitive views is that they protect us from mystery and imagination, and I would argue, protect us from the fullness of what salvation is and does. (More about this below.) If we take, as we should, salvation to be more than the cross, we will understand the nature and purpose of Christ's sacrifice primarily from the standpoint of Christ and not sacrifice. That is, we do not take a definition, understanding, or particular history of sacrifice and attach it to Christ's death on the cross. While we cannot ignore this history, since its currents helped bring about the event itself (Jesus was not the only person the Romans crucified), we need to explore what the cross is within the whole of Christ's life and within the whole scope of theology. Christ's saving work is all of Christ and his work: incarnation, ministry and sayings, death, resurrection, ascension, and second coming along with the sending of the Holy Spirit. In this way, soteriological questions become Eucharistic ones.

Similarly, from the Eucharist side of the equation, we must attend to all types and dimensions of offering or sacrifice that occur within the Eucharist and as Eucharist. While we may privilege one or two moments or actions of the Eucharistic liturgy as the sacrifice or offering, an awareness of how the whole celebration is imbued with offering is required. The celebration of the Eucharist is a kaleidoscope of actions opening out toward a panorama of sacrificial vision. Gathering, confessing, proclaiming, listening, praying, offering, sharing, remembering, invoking, praising, giving, and receiving are all acts of dispossession for the sake of a life beyond ourselves, for a relationship that we cannot create or produce.

Turning directly to the question whether the Eucharist is a sacrifice, different avenues are taken to answer this question with a yes or an no. The primary referent for the sacrificial nature or purpose of the Eucharist can be the sacrifice of Christ. The relationship between cross and Eucharist is determinative. Note the regular use of the words "nature" and "purpose." The Eucharist could be considered not to have a sacrificial nature but a sacrificial purpose. It is not a sacrifice itself, nor does a sacrifice happen within it, but its performance is a restoration, reconciliation, or renewal of a saving relationship with God. The sacrifice of Christ makes possible the sacrificial purpose of the Eucharist even though by nature the Eucharist is not a sacrifice. Likewise, there can be a distinction between saying the Eucharist is a sacrifice or is sacrificial. We could say that the Eucharist has such a close relationship to Christ's sacrifice that it shares in its sacrificial nature and purpose without being a distinct sacrificial act.

The Eucharist can be a sacrifice or sacrificial due to the sacrifice or offering made by the people gathered. They could offer the sacrifice of praise, of thanksgiving, of "ourselves, our souls and bodies" (a phrase from traditional Anglican Eucharistic prayers). The assembly could offer the bread and wine, or they could offer Christ as he is sacramentally present in the bread and wine. The primary referent for the sacrificial nature of the Eucharist here is not what Christ has done but what the people do. The avenue to an absolute negative answer to the question of Eucharist and sacrifice would say that we cannot offer or sacrifice anything to God, even ourselves, lest we give any hint that our actions assist or merit our salvation. Another referent for the sacrificial nature and purpose of the Eucharist is not the cross but Christ's priesthood; not what he has done but what he is doing.

Assessment of the sacrificial nature and purpose of the Eucharist takes place from two viewpoints: one historical and the other heavenly. The cross is an event in history; it has a location in time and place, and consists of a particular set of actions. These actions have received normative theological interpretations and meanings. History is not just what happened, but is an attempt to say why it happened and what it means then and now. Likewise, the Eucharist is an event in history; it happens at a given place and time as a set of normative and recognizable actions. A correspondence between two historical events can be established through repetitive action—we do what was done—and/or through duplicative meaning—it means what it meant. One way in which this correspondence has been made is to view the relationship between the cross as Christ's sacrifice and the Eucharist through the actions and meaning of the Last Supper. Christ offered himself in bread and wine so that his offering on the cross can be effectively available to us in our offering of him in bread and wine.

The Last Supper and the Eucharist form a set of salvific bookends around the cross. Jesus' words over the bread, and especially over the cup, are bound to the meaning of the cross so that the repetition of these words always involves his sacrifice. The institution narrative is not only Eucharistic words but crucifixion words; they share the same history and make the same history possible. According to this perspective, the saving effectiveness of Christ's sacrifice on the cross, mediated by the words and actions of the Last Supper, becomes temporally transcendent.

A different view of the relationship between Last Supper, cross, and Eucharist guards their historical location. The event belongs to its own time and place and to no other. History is a series of events rather than a continuum of consequences. The sufficiency of the cross—a once-for-all sacrifice—depends upon an absolute uniqueness: not only will it not happen again, it cannot happen again in any way. The Eucharist too is something that happens now for now; it is always effectively contemporary. The gaps of history are bridged not by sharing reality or common activity but by a receptiveness of the present to the past and by a consciousness of memorial. We do something because something else was done by someone else; we do not do the same thing in a different way. The events of the past belong solely to their enacting agents. Different agents mean different events. For this view of history, the sacrificial nature and purpose of the cross cannot belong to the Eucharist.

The separation of cross and Eucharist does not preclude any sacrificial connotations for the latter. As we saw with Luther, a heavenly horizon, instead of an historical one, regards the Eucharistic actions of offering as a reaching up and not as a reaching back. The offering of praise, thanksgiving, and selves to Christ is directed toward heaven where he is the high priest interceding for us (Hebrews 4:14–16). The heavenly orientation of the Eucharistic sacrifice allows for the "offering of the heavenly Christ" in contrast to "offering the historical Christ." It is a vertical movement more than a horizontal one. The heavenly horizon is present as well when making an offering of Christ to the Father through a shared imagery between the church's altar and the heavenly altar. The Roman Canon puts it this way:

> We humbly beseech you, almighty God, bid these things be borne by the hands of your angel to your altar on high, in the sight of your divine majesty, that all of us who have received the most holy

body and blood of your Son by partaking at this altar may be filled with all heavenly blessing and grace; through Christ our Lord.[14]

There is the offering to Christ in heaven and the offering of Christ to the Father in heaven.

The contrast between a causal and a participatory dynamic generates various understandings of the efficaciousness of the Eucharist as a sacrifice or as sacrificial. The dynamic of cause and effect resonates with the historical perspective, while a participatory one is more conducive to the heavenly perspective. We can begin with the normative and abiding statement that Christ's death on the cross was a sacrifice for the forgiveness of sins: His death causes the effect of the remission of sins. Is this effect perpetual without another cause? The Reformed view maintains the singular cause with its enduring effect. The Roman Catholic view holds that the primal cause is renewed by further causative action (the sacrifice of the Mass). In order for there to be the effect of the forgiveness of sins as an actual event in someone's life, this person requires an accompanying causal event: the Mass said for the living and the dead. Since the cross, there has been a series of linear causes with assigned effects. The similarities drawn between cross and Eucharist are similarities of causes and effects as well as of actions and meanings. An inherent aspect of cause and effect mutuality is the assignment of a particular effect to a particular cause. This cause produces this effect. Theologically, we could well ask whether a causal understanding of the Eucharist is always or ever appropriate or adequate? We could say it is appropriate but never adequate.

What happens in the Eucharist? What are the consequences of its celebration? One fundamental approach to answering these kinds of questions is to understand the Eucharist as, above all, a participatory event. The Eucharist participates in, or shares, a reality not its own. All of the Eucharistic actions are not meant to produce or cause anything; they are enacted as a form of availability and expectation. The actions are oriented toward reception of God's presence and will. The horizon of Eucharistic effectiveness is not so much what comes after its celebration, but what precedes and surrounds it. Put another way, the Eucharist is not primarily an act that justifies the sinner but a sacrament of heaven. The primal movement is not what it does to us but where it takes us. While a cause and effect relationship emphasizes that something is indeed done, the participatory sensibility insists that more is done than we think or understand: "Now to him who by the power at work within us is able to accomplish abundantly far more than all we can ask or imagine" (Ephesians 3:20). As participation in the saving reality of Christ, the accountable referent of the Eucharist is not solely the "what" or "when" of the cross but the "who" and "why" of Christ.

Another formative relationship within the Eucharistic economy is between presence and sacrifice. The Roman exposition of this relationship speaks of Christ's presence preceding his offering: In order for Christ to be truly offered he must be really present. The institution narrative in the Roman Canon is regarded as the moment when Christ becomes present as the bread and wine, and the offering of these gifts becomes the offering of him. Christ is present within our agency; we can do something with him, even though we would add that he is also there to do something with and for us. From the other side of this debate, if Christ is not there within our agency, we certainly cannot offer him. We can only offer what is in our hands and what is subject to our will. Our understanding of sacrifice is predicated on our belief in Christ's presence. In scholastic theology, the Eucharist is treated as sacrament and as sacrifice, as an event of Christ's presence and his saving work. However, sacrament and sacrifice are not separate theological spheres because Christ's person and work are not: Christ's presence in the Eucharist is his work.

Who does what in the Eucharist and why? A great deal of our theological attention is focused on what we do, can do, or should do. While we may give a nod to divine agency, we focus on the sacramental maneuverings of human agency, particularly those performed by authorized and ordained agents. The Roman Catholic teaching that we have reviewed portrays a cooperation between divine and human agency. For the Reformers, whether they permit any human agency or not, when it comes to salvation, divine agency is singular, absolute, and ultimate. God's activity demands our faithful passivity and does not require any activity on our part for its effectiveness. The problem for the Reformers was their assessment that the Mass had become a work, an act of human agents. Again, what kind of presence of Christ is there in the Eucharist? Is he present from afar (heavenly), present within (sacramental), or as the gathering (ecclesial)? What is the purpose of this presence? Is it an active or passive presence? The question of human agency becomes: What do we do because of what Christ has done, is doing, or will do? How do we act before the Eucharistic presence of Christ?

EUCHARISTIC SALVATION

Asking whether the Eucharist is a sacrifice or not, and if it is, what kind of sacrifice, is to pose a question in the middle of a conversation. All of the basic subjects and topics of theology form the context, the appropriate conversation, for asking and answering this question. The whole scope of theological vision is either explicitly or implicitly invested in Eucharistic theology of any sort, and this is certainly the case when considering the relationship between the celebration of the Eucharist and the sacrifice of Christ on the cross. In order to make an adequate beginning in the effort to transcend and to transform the customary terms of the debate, let us entertain the nature of the cross as a theological point of departure.

> For the message about the cross is foolishness to those who are perishing, but to us who are being saved it is the power of God. For it is written, "I will destroy the wisdom of the wise, and the discernment of the discerning I will thwart." Where is the one who is wise? Where is the scribe? Where is the debater of this age? Has not God made foolish the wisdom of this world? For since, in the wisdom of God, the world did not know God through wisdom. God decided, through the foolishness of our proclamation, to save those who believe. For Jews demand signs and Greeks desire wisdom, but we proclaim Christ crucified, a stumbling-block to Jews and foolishness to Gentiles, but to those who are the called, both Jews and Greeks, Christ the power of God and the wisdom of God. (1 Corinthians 1:18–24)

The cross is not supposed to make sense; it cannot be conceptually apprehended by our customary strategies of explanation and justification. The cross is a mystery of God's wisdom. Mystery does not mean something that is always confusing; it is not a euphemism for obfuscation. Mystery is an invitation to draw closer to what God would show us and to what God would have us understand. Mystery is a type of knowing that belongs to those who are called to be Christ's body. The mystery of the cross is wisely garnered by a baptismal epistemology. Prior to being a mystery we are called to inhabit, the cross is an event of Jesus; it is a Christological reality.

The whole of Jesus' life was a handing over of self to the Father, to do what the Father sent him to do. That is, Jesus lived sacrificially before he died sacrificially. His identity and vocation was an exercise of *kenosis* (Philippians 2:5–11). Jesus is an offering of the Father's to us, and he to the Father and to us. Therefore, the cross is a pivotal and defining event of an offering life, but it is not the only moment of sacrifice. The cross opens up for us a vista of offering, a rich and multidimensional complex of sacrifice. The cross cannot have a *sui generis* theology. It is a dimension of the whole sweep of salvation that flows into the world in the person and history of Christ blown along by the power of the Holy Spirit. The incarnation is an offering of God and the resurrection is the destiny of our offering to God. The economy of salvation is an array of mutuality and gift, a comprehensive invitation to enter Christ's life of communion.

We receive this invitation in the Eucharist; the Eucharist is our yes to Christ's life of communion. As such, the connection between the cross and the Eucharist is located within the broader apprehension of the fullness of salvation. In this way, the words and actions of Jesus at the Last Supper are not regarded solely as the institution of the Eucharist. They become the binding promise between his sacrificial life and the life offered in the celebration of the Eucharist, the life offered to us and our offering of life. What happens in the Eucharist is what happens to him, through him, with him, and by him. The commandment to "Do this in remembrance of me" creates a place for a human agency that is not directed toward itself—its accomplishments and satisfactions—but toward its own redemption. There is now a way to act redemptively within the place made possible by the memory of Jesus and his redemptive history and agency. As examined above, many Eucharistic prayers follow the memorial injunction with a recounting of Christ's saving events, which lead to an offering of the people. The Eucharistic prayer from the *Liturgy of St. James* moves from "Do this for my remembrance" to "we offer you, Master, this awesome and bloodless sacrifice" with this memorial passage:

> remembering his life—giving sufferings and his saving cross and his death and his burial and his Resurrection from the dead on the third day and his return to heaven and his session at your right hand, his God and Father, and his glorious and awesome second coming.[15]

Here we have a fulsome remembrance of the saving history of Christ, including an event from the future. Entering into the remembrance of Christ is participation in his history beyond the bounds of our own. Our agency becomes his work; our striving becomes his accomplishment.

The cross exists within the mystery of salvation and the Eucharist is an act of the church; the juncture between the Christological Body of Christ and the ecclesial Body of Christ is baptism. When reflecting on the relationship between divine and human agency in the Eucharistic economy, we are talking about baptismal agency. The main objection to the Eucharist as a sacrifice is rooted in a two-fold division between divine agency and human agency, between the cross and humanity. Christ's sacrifice on the cross is sufficient for our salvation, understood primarily as forgiveness of sins, and we can only receive its benefits as an act of God. As humans, we are sinners and unworthy to offer God anything that would "merit" salvation. Our actions are kept separate from God's actions. From the Roman Catholic side of the debate, the relationship between divine and human agency is cooperative; God's saving actions have made our sacramental actions possible. The Eucharistic action becomes a saving one, and our theological focus shifts toward an arbitration of what we do and to what effect. Is there another way to approach the relationship between divine and human agency besides complete division or cooperation?

Baptism is being incorporated into the Body of Christ and receiving the gift of the Holy Spirit. Baptism transfers people from the circumscribed sphere of human agency to the place, and into the person, where human agency is taken up into the divine agency; where they are distinct but not separated. Christians are buried into Christ's death, and consequently, "So you also must consider yourselves dead to sin and alive to God in Christ Jesus" (Romans 6:11). We are baptized into Christ's agency, which is never an individual exercise of the will nor a program for self-development or self-aggrandizement of any sort. Christ always sought to do the will of the Father, and he relied on the Spirit to perform it. Divine agency is Trinitarian; it is the mutuality and cooperation of three persons. One person does not act alone; the act of one is the act of all, even though they might not all act in the same way. Baptismal agency is the human exercise of Trinitarian agency. It is always an act with and toward, an abiding movement among persons: the *perichoresis* of agency.

We are baptized into Christ's offering life, so that maturity in Christ will develop through an ongoing dynamic of offering and of sacrifice: the passage from the old to the new agency. The Eucharist is celebrated by the gathering of baptismal agents. The Eucharistic economy entails a communion of agency. What is done in the Eucharist and as Eucharist happens through the Trinitarian sharing of agency among the divine persons, and through the invitation issued to baptismal agents to act within, toward, and as the communion into which they were buried. This is the mystery of Trinitarian agency that is properly the subject of contemplation and not analysis. In this way, divine agency is for recognition more than for protection. However, there are caveats to the exercise of baptismal agency within the economy of the Eucharist: It will always be an exchange of gift, and not a purchase of possession; it will be an act of expectation and not calculation; and it will be for the realization of communion and not individual improvement.

While the role of agency is key to the question of Eucharist and sacrifice, the comprehensive theological context is salvation or redemption. If we understand salvation as a singular reality brought about by a particular act, then we will either find a similar and corresponding act in the Eucharist or we will not. One could say, "You do this and say this to be saved" or, "This is how one enters into the status of being saved." However, if salvation is not so much a singular act nor a state of being, but a complex of actions and an emerging life (sanctification), then the question of what performance(s) and habits reflect and realize salvation will be more expansive and probing. Salvation will be multidimensional and so will be its enacted and expressive life.

We have acknowledged that how Christ's presence in the Eucharist is viewed shapes convictions about the place and role of sacrifice or offering by the participants. However, Christ's presence has a nature and a purpose; he is actively there, and not there to be acted upon. Christ is present in the Eucharist offering the baptized his life of communion. The specificity of "his life" is crucial. Christ's history of communion is what is remembered, and it is this history that makes the baptismal response possible. Christ is not present without his history, but the purpose of this history is to make another history possible. This is why Eucharistic *anamnesis* or memorial is not an exercise of imitation, repetition, or recollection. The invocation of the Holy Spirit over baptismal offering is the breaking in of salvation. Salvation happens with our *kenotic* response to Christ's invitation to enter into his life of communion. Salvation happens as communion and for communion. The cross of Christ is a dimension of this history to which we are placed by baptism, and in which we faithfully inhabit in Eucharist. The cross is an icon into the gaze of Christ's communion. Christ's sacrifice is his entry into that place where all becomes what God would have it to be: sacrament, resurrection, and the new creation. The Eucharist is following Christ from cross to tomb to resurrection and to heaven and back again with the promise of finality and fulfillment.

Salvation as communion, as mutuality of agents inhabiting Christ's life, leads to a multidimensional appreciation of the whole complex of expressions and actions that constitute the celebration of the Eucharist: Its enactment is adequate to the life for which it exists. While there are moments of clarity regarding offering, the whole complex of actions shares in, and reflects, the primal baptismal movement of sacrifice, of handing over ourselves as gifts for communion with God and with each other in Christ and by the Holy Spirit. The Eucharist is a communion of actions and of selves that remain distinct and mutually available to each other. The celebration of the Eucharist is sacrificial because communion is sacrificial both in performance and in reality.

CHAPTER 4

CHURCH

The cup of blessing that we bless, is it not a sharing in the blood of Christ? The bread that we break, is it not a sharing in the body of Christ? Because there is one bread, we who are many are one body, for we all partake of the one bread.

1 Corinthians 10:16–17

The Eucharist as tradition, presence, and sacrifice will not be fully appreciated without reflecting on Eucharist as church. It is the church that celebrates the Eucharist; it is not an optional behavior of individual Christians. The Eucharist is inherently a corporate exercise and event. This means that Eucharistic questions are ineluctably ecclesiological questions. The church's nature, authority, ministry, polity, and mission will be somehow implicated in the performance and understanding of its Eucharistic celebration. In fact, often a rethinking and redoing of the nature and activity of the church will be directed toward changing the liturgy to express and proclaim this reform. The Eucharist is viewed as a means to achieve a church mandate or mission. In this way, the Eucharist is understood as one of various activities and might be called into service for the greater good of what the church is and wishes to do. Examples would include Eucharistic liturgies promoting inclusivity, diversity, multiculturalism, church growth, social justice, the needs of the young or of families, or to assuage the anxious in a time of rapid change. In and of themselves, all of these concerns are worthy of our ecclesial attention, but should the Eucharistic liturgy be the means of addressing them? The answer to this question resides within our basic normative understanding of the Eucharist and of the church, and especially, within our understanding of the relationship between them: an Eucharistic ecclesia and an ecclesial Eucharist.

Rather than viewing the Eucharist as something the church does, or one of an array of activities, we could approach the church from the Eucharist. The Eucharist is the event of the church; the church is the event of the Eucharist. The mutuality between church and Eucharist is such that we cannot, or should not, theologically approach one without full regard for the other. We could go even further and say that not only are church and Eucharist inseparable, but that the Eucharist is the primary and paradigmatic manifestation of what and why the church exists. This is quite a claim, and this chapter will be devoted to its exposition. Before proceeding with this, we need to address some difficult ecclesial facts.

All the churches that have celebrations of the Eucharist, both those churches that do this occasionally and those that do it every Sunday, do not all affirm the Eucharistic character of others as their own. We could say that there are as many Eucharists, Eucharistic types, as there are churches. Not all churches allow nonmembers to receive communion. Not all churches recognize the "validity" of other church's ordained ministry, and consequently, they question whether what happens in one church is the same as what happens in theirs. Even in the age of "substantial" ecumenical agreements on the doctrine of the Eucharist among churches, the actual celebration of it can, and does, serve as a sign of disunity, something that points in the opposite direction as the sacramental character of the Eucharist itself.

A survey of all Christian churches would show that some of them do not regard the Eucharist as central to their nature and purpose and do not have a complete and normative ritual. They might have a truncated "Lord's Supper" but not have all of the actions that constitute the Eucharistic celebration from the gathering to the dismissal. These churches do have elements of their life that also have a place in the Eucharist, e.g., reading Scripture and praying for others. Different churches and their liturgical life and theology should not be homogenized into a grand and universal concept of church that ignores or relativizes the particulars of each one. However, a common ecclesial life will have some common ways of living together and not just a few observed parallels between churches. The perspective guiding the following exposition of the formative relationship between Eucharist and church takes the Eucharist as foundational to the church's nature and purpose. As such, those churches that do not fit this profile are not directly considered but are implicated.

Furthermore, the presumption here is that the Eucharist is the necessary center from which, and to which, all ecclesial reality should conform and be transformed.

In order to gain a better appreciation of the formative relationship between church and Eucharist, we will reflect first on ways of understanding the church that do not directly incorporate the Eucharist. A basic operative distinction in understanding the church, an ecclesiology, is between the church's nature and purpose: what it is and what it does. So, for instance, the church could be designated by a set of nouns: Body of Christ, people of God, or people of the New Covenant. Or, it could be approached principally as an institution or corporate entity that resides in a specific identity. When speaking of churches, this identity and naming reflects some distinctive form of polity or central dogma, e.g., Methodist, Episcopal, Presbyterian, or Baptist. Or, instead, the purpose of the church can be the primary way to account for its existence. The church exists to proclaim the Word of God, to serve the world's needs, to work for social justice, or to provide a spiritual oasis for secular lives. Whether an ecclesiology gravitates toward nature or purpose, this perspective becomes comprehensive, whereby all of the church's life is accounted for in this way, or a renewal is instigated on these terms. Sometimes, a church, local or universal, might attempt to recall an aspect of its nature and purpose that has been submerged or forgotten. A current example would be mission. Churches or various juridical bodies, such as dioceses or presbyteries, attempt to re-conceive and direct their whole self-perception and work around the theme of mission.

A closer examination of various ecclesiologies, or customary approaches to church or churches, reflects an array of emphases located within the arenas of nature and purpose. One can focus on what the church teaches; how its doctrines inform and shape its life and seeks to do the same for everyone. The church is identified by its teaching within the scope of its polity as well as directed to the public. Teaching moves from within to without. Another basic movement is characterized by belief: from without to within. This movement ushers persons into not only believing certain things, or a set of beliefs, but believing in God or Jesus. Belief is personal: this is what I believe or what we believe. We become aware of ourselves as those who believe or as believers. Herein lies another ecclesial distinction: the act of believing and the content of belief. The determinative factor might be what is believed, or it might be believing. In a post-modern context that shies away from grand narratives, universal truths, bridging differences, and normative language, any one-to-one correspondence between a personal act or sentiment and an exterior reality is avoided. We become a "person of faith" who may or may not belong to a "community of faith." An abstraction is nurtured in order to move away from the concrete reality of a particular church with a particular set of beliefs that would lay a claim on one's own particularity. Sometimes, a church might be a gathering reflective of prior gathering, e.g. family or community. The church is another way for groups of persons to gather, who have other important gather-ings: Here is one more instance of a gathering of this group of gath-erers. These church gatherings might have an articulated theme for gathering, e.g. faith, hope, or love.

If the content of belief is the determinative factor of church life, then belonging would be constituted by adhering to content, which is to be learned and/or obeyed. The recognition of fellow members of the church, and being recognized as a member of this church, is delineated by certain binding beliefs. One cannot be a member of this church unless this belief or set of beliefs is held. There can be a hier-archy of beliefs, with some being central and necessary, while oth-ers are secondary and indifferent. The demarcation point between what is central and what is secondary itself becomes an ecclesial or denominational trait. A church keenly aware of its identity residing in beliefs will protect its borders with the world, and perhaps, with other churches.

Amid an array of understandings and practices emerging from attending to the nature and purpose of the church or churches, can we, or should we, identify a normative and accountable ecclesiol-ogy? Answering this question pertains to our frame of reference, to the principal question that generates the question of church. This generative question is appropriately referred to God; it is a theologi-cal question. What is God's will for humanity, for the world, for its redemptive gathering? How is this will an expression of God's nature? What is the nature and purpose of Jesus? How did he provide for the ongoing gathering of his disciples to not only be with each other, but to be with him, to be gathered into his life? The question of church is the question of God, of Jesus, and of salvation; it is a vision of a new humanity born from the baptismal font into the Eucharistic gather-ing of heaven and earth.

THE EUCHARIST MAKES THE CHURCH

Jesus' words and actions at the Last Supper are not only the origins of the institution of the Eucharist but of the church as well. After the resurrection and ascension of Jesus, and the descent of the Holy Spirit, the followers of Jesus would assemble as the church; the church is this assembly of Christians. Furthermore, the regular gathering of Christians as church was the celebration of the Eucharist. The church begins as the Eucharistic assembly. The primitive experience and existence as church, and of being a member of the church, was bounded and formed by the event of the Eucharist. The leadership and teaching of the church were the leaders and teachers at the Eucharist. Oversight of the Eucharist and of the church were the same ministry. The life of the early Christians, of the early church, was a Eucharistic one. When someone was made a Christian at baptism, they were brought into the assembly to join in the prayers of the people and to stay for the Eucharistic prayer and communion. This was the first time they were present and participated in the full celebration of the Eucharist; from that point on they belonged to those who gather for Eucharist. After baptism and their first Eucharist, the new Christians would be taught the meaning of what had happened, and what happened to them. Teaching was a reflective exercise on something already seen, heard, and experienced. Much of our knowledge of baptism and Eucharist from the primitive church comes from the records of these teachings. Eucharist, Christian, and church are inseparable realities in the first few centuries of their mutual existence.

The church as lived from, and understood by, the celebration of the Eucharist has been rendered succinctly by the phrase, "the Eucharist makes the church." This phrase first appears in the course of a study of the application of the "mystical body of Christ" to the Eucharist and then to the church. In his book, *Corpus Mysticum: The Eucharist and the Church in the Middle Ages*, Henri de Lubac traces the use of "*corpus mysticum*" in patristic and medieval theological literature, and finds that the appellation "mystical body" shifts from the Eucharist to the church, while the phrase "true body" of Christ shifts from church to the Eucharist. The church becomes the mystical body of Christ, and the Eucharist contains the "true body" of Christ. De Lubac's summary statement on the relationship between the Eucharist and the church as generative is as follows:

> Now, the Eucharist is the mystical principle, permanently at work at the heart of Christian society, which gives concrete form to this miracle. It is the universal bond, it is the ever-springing source of life. Nourished by the body and blood of the Saviour, his faithful people thus all 'drink of the one Spirit,' who truly makes them into one single body. Literally speaking, therefore, the Eucharist makes the Church. It makes of it an inner reality. By its hidden power, the members of the body come to unite themselves by becoming more fully members of Christ, and their unity with one another is part and parcel of their unity with one single Head.[1]

The Eucharist lies deep within the church's life as its animating principle; it is the church's "heart" that continues to pump life throughout the body. This "ever-springing source of life" abides within the church as an event that offers both continuity and renewal; the Eucharist forms the church. The reason for this is not because the celebration of the Eucharist is an ecclesial end unto itself. It is the event when and where Christ's faithful people are fed by his body and blood and united by the Spirit. The profound encounter between Christ and his Spirit-gathered followers unifies them. They grow closer together as they grow closer to Christ.

The formative relationship between Eucharist and church is not just in one direction: from Eucharist to church. The church exists beyond the liturgical enactment of the Eucharist, and not everything that the church is and does is directly Eucharistic. There are distinctions residing within this relationship, which can serve to foster an enduring vibrancy. For de Lubac, "The Church and the Eucharist are formed by one another day by day: the idea of the Church and the idea of the Eucharist must promote one another mutually and each be rendered more profound by the other."[2] The Eucharist and the church are reforming forces for each other as they are oriented toward each other. An Eucharistic ecclesia will seek to become more Eucharistic, while an ecclesial Eucharist will seek to become more ecclesial.

The image of an ongoing nurturing vitality between church and Eucharist is more adequately appreciated by acknowledging that this is more a call for renewal than a description of the status quo. De

Lubac's study depicts the transition from "the Eucharist makes the church" to "the church makes the Eucharist." Over time, the Eucharist becomes one of the acts of the church, something it does by its own authority stemming from outside the celebration. The basic and normative theology of church is constructed from other places with ends other than the theological account of the nature and purpose of the Eucharist. A theology of grace, of salvation, and a juridical view of the institutional church can become the interpretative context for the Eucharist. The Eucharist now is a way for the church to accomplish its ends, or a way to apply a content located elsewhere. This theological bifurcation between church and Eucharist distorts them both to an extent where they become blinders and not ways to view the deeper call in each to Christ's bid to live in him.

If the Eucharist makes the church and always has an ecclesial existence, then we are confronted with the challenge of a common life. Our heightened awareness of difference among people, a strong individualism, a consumer culture of branding, and market research that identifies or creates personal needs all pose a considerable challenge to any attempt to inhabit a common life. All of the ways that we identify ourselves culturally, economically, socially, politically, and even religiously can be obstacles to a Eucharistic and ecclesial common life. Do we assemble our identities or is the assembly our identity? Is the church an aggregate of people or is it a people? The answer to these questions begins with whether we have a keen sense of baptism as a passage from one life to another, from individuality to commonality, from secular to sacred, from world to church, and from liturgies of sameness to the Eucharist.

The church does not exist except as the common life of Christians, and Christians do not exist authentically and fully except as a common life. In other words, we are faced with the challenge of separation. We can separate the church from Christians and vice versa by presuming some kind of independent life among them, which is connected to each other from time to time. One goes to church instead of being the church, or the church is something persons like to support because of how it has helped them. We have grown very accustomed to all sorts of separation, of ways to maintain lives distinguished by individual traits and successes or failures. Who I am is my nature, which is a self-referential construct with stress on the "my." In the area of the will, I am my choice; life is what I choose it to be, or is a product of several choices over time. The challenge of a common life is also a theological one.

We can separate Christ from church, church from Eucharist, and Eucharist from life. Each can be understood within a framework that does not implicate the other: Christ is who he is, the church is what it is, and I am who I am. Contrast this series of statements with Christ is what the church is, the church is who Christ is, I am what the church is, and the Eucharist is who Christ, church, and we are. We have the dilemma of a common life that is not comprised of a singular identity nor of several divisible identities. Jesus is not an individual apart from the second person of the Trinity, from his disciples, from the Christ, from the baptized, from the church, and apart from his sacrificial presence in the Eucharist. Christians are not individuals apart from Christ, from the Triune God, from the church, from the Eucharist, nor even apart from each other.

A compelling insight into the Eucharist as the common life of Christians is given by the account of the martyrdom of St. Saturninus and his companions in Carthage in 304 AD.

"These persons, being Christians, have held an assembly for the Eucharist, contrary to the edict of Emperors Diocletian and Maximian." So read the charge made by the magistrates of the town of Abitina in North Africa. "What is your rank?" inquired the proconsul Anulinus of the first prisoner presented to him. "I am a senator," replied Dativus. "Were you present in the assembly?" "I am a Christian and I was present in the assembly." Straightway the proconsul ordered him to be suspended on the rack and his body torn by the barbed hooks. Then Saturninus, the priest, was arraigned for combat. The proconsul asked, "Did you, contrary to the orders of emperors, arrange for these persons to hold an assembly?" Saturninus replied, "Certainly. We celebrated the Eucharist." "Why?" "Because the Eucharist cannot be abandoned." As soon as he said this, the proconsul ordered him to be put immediately on the rack with Dativus. Then Felix, a son of Saturninus and a reader of the Church, came forward to the contest. Whereupon the proconsul inquired of him, "I am not asking you if you are a Christian. You can hold your peace about that! But were you one of the assembly; and do you possess any copies of the Scriptures?" Felix answered, "As if a Christian could exist without the Eucharist, or the Eucharist be celebrated without the Christian! Don't you know that a Christian is constituted by the Eucharist, and the Eucharist by a Christian? Neither avails without the other."[3]

Standing in the way of such a vision are several other modes of Christian identity or identification. These modes are often associated with values or spiritual sensibilities or practices. One might refer to oneself as "Christian" but not "a Christian," thus regarding the appellation of Christian as a trait or an opinion about certain religious topics. One could assign the Christian noun to oneself without being associated with any defined group of Christians. What is missing is an identity and life that exists authoritatively outside of the self to which the self is initiated and hence transformed. What is missing is the habitual belonging to the Eucharistic assembly and all of its requisite disciplines.

The common life that is woven by the mutuality of Eucharist and church, and into which Christians are placed, re-arranges how we customarily regard the pairing of objective and subjective. The modern period of epistemology, beginning in the seventeenth century with Descartes, exalted the subject as the center of knowledge rather than what is known. The knower becomes the arbiter of knowledge; knowledge is not the self-evident property of the known. Through methods of reasoning pertaining to all types of knowledge, the knower enters upon the quest to say something true and timeless about an identified object. Subjects approach objects as something over against themselves whose nature can be deciphered by the appropriate procedures. The more we became aware of the complexity of subjects and of subjectivity, the more complex our appreciation of what it means to know and of what there is to know. When the center of gravity shifted in the subject from reason to experience in the twentieth century, the greater sense of subjectivity as distinctive of the subject took hold. Instead of a path to objectivity, the subject's own subjectivity is revealed. Our experience of the world becomes our world and not yours, and your experience is your world and not ours. Through our subjectivity we build epistemological homes for ourselves where no alien reality may dwell. We domesticate objects; they belong in our home, or they do not belong.

The subjectivity of our construals of reality bestows upon us an array of objects which we can choose either as relationships or possessions. We can choose what kind of relationship we might have, and what we wish to own. We objectify our world. This economy of subject and object, and its attendant ethic of choice, is inverted by the Eucharistic church and its common life. Membership in the church is a subjective belonging that objectifies you, making you a Christian. Our Eucharistic subjectivity issues from a common life that forms who we are and directs us to certain authentic and appropriate choices. The Eucharist makes the church that makes Christians. Who I am belongs to who we are, gathered for the sacrificial presence of Christ in communion. In this economy, objects are gifts and subjects are recipients. The church is the normative event and life where and how this exchange happens.

Another, and more directly theological, approach to the common life that is the Eucharistic church is the contrast between character and communion. In the Scholastic period, character was a concept employed to speak of the enduring and distinctive reality of a sacrament. There is the character of ordination that is an interior stamp or mark that establishes one as a priest forever. Once a character has been given, it is not something that can go away. The root of this notion can be traced back to the patristic idea that one is branded or marked as belonging to Christ in baptism. For our purposes, character is something that resides within someone; this is who that person is, and then they live and act according to this identity. The ontology of character moves from within to without. In contrast, the ontology of communion is a movement from without to within. You are who you are because of an identifying relationship. Ordination places someone in a specific relational place within the common life of the church. It is one's place within the common life that makes you who you are. Identity has a corporate perspective. This is why an ordained person as well as anyone who is baptized is a person of and in the church: an identity of and from communion. What leads the way in the church's life is not what belongs to an individual, e.g. power, will, thought, or conscience, but what already belongs to everyone. The Eucharist is a corporate action and life that is manifested in the diversity of those assembled. Communion is unity without sameness and difference without alienation. Subjects of communion do not become objects of competition. The Eucharist makes the church into the common life of communion.

A powerful exponent of the generative relationship between the Eucharist and the church was Augustine of Hippo. In several of his sermons, biblical commentaries and other texts, he exhorts and elaborates the vital and definitive connection between what happens in the Eucharist and what happens to the baptized. In a particularly vivid account offered in a sermon on Easter Sunday (Sermon 227), Augustine addresses those who were baptized the night before at the Easter Vigil. Commenting on the text "We who are many are one body, for we all partake of the same bread" (1 Corinthians 10:17), he tells his listeners that they should regard themselves as this bread. He draws a parallel between how bread is made and how persons become Christians. The bread is made from many grains that are pounded together, mixed with water, and treated with fire. This is how many grains become one loaf of bread. Likewise, the newly baptized were many different people who through fasting and exorcisms were pounded together in preparation for baptism. At baptism the water was added, and then they were anointed with oil, which represents the fire of the Holy Spirit. Baptism makes many different people into the one loaf of bread, the one Body of Christ.

For Augustine, the identity between the bread of the Eucharist and membership in the church is as the Body of Christ: the mutuality between the sacramental and ecclesial Body. This identity is not something added to individuals or to a group, but who they are completely and are called to become. In another sermon, Augustine states:

> The body of Christ cannot live but by the Spirit of Christ. It is for this that the Apostle Paul, expounding the bread, says: 'One bread,' saith he, 'we being many are one body.' O mystery of piety! O sign of unity! O bond of charity! He that would live has where to live, has whence to live. Let him draw near, let him believe, let him be embodied, that he may be made to live.[4]

He argues that just as a human body lives by its spirit, the Body of Christ lives by the Spirit of Christ. As members of the Body of Christ, the baptized are to live by the Spirit of Christ, which is what animates this life into a living reality. The Body of Christ is visible, while the Spirit of Christ is invisible; it is the hidden principle that shapes the baptized into what they have been made. The Body of Christ is both a place to belong and a way to live.

As a bishop and pastor, Augustine knew well that being baptized did not guarantee full Christian maturity and holiness of life. He would tell his listeners to strive to live into the life that has been bestowed in baptism and comprised by the Eucharist. The celebration of the Eucharist was a regular reminder of the Christian's identity and accountability, of what it means to be the Body of Christ. In one sermon, Augustine exhorts the assembly thus:

> So if it's you that are the body of Christ and its members, it's the mystery meaning you that has been placed on the Lord's table;

what you receive is the mystery that means you. It is what you are that you reply Amen by so replying you express your assent. What you hear, you see, is the body of Christ, and you answer, Amen. So be members of the body of Christ in order to make that Amen true.[5]

For an Eucharistic ecclesiology, which he conveys, the normative image of the church is as the Body of Christ. An ecclesiology contrived from this image will shape all ecclesial questions and issues. That is, one does not just state that the church is the Body of Christ, and then proceed to consider everything else within a different paradigm. As noted above, there are different theologies of, and sensibilities about, the church or churches. Before turning directly to an exposition of the Eucharistic church, we will spend a little more time with what it means to be the Body of Christ.

In various texts of the New Testament, the church is identified as the Body of Christ with Christ as its head (Colossians 1:18, 24). The appeal to being the Body of Christ becomes the basis for describing how the life and ministry of the church is varied and mutually dependent (Romans 12:4–5). The members of the body need each other to be and do who they are for the body to be and do what it is. Paul puts it this way:

For just as the body is one and has many members, and all the members of the body, though many, are one body, so it is with Christ. For in the one Spirit we were all baptized into one body— Jews or Greeks, slaves or free—and we were all made to drink of one Spirit. Indeed, the body does not consist of one member but of many. (1 Corinthians 12: 12–14)

The Body of Christ is not a piecing together of similar parts; there is not a prior natural semblance that allows the members to coexist as one. Instead, the one Spirit makes what otherwise are separate bodies into one body. The Spirit is not bound by nature or history; it forms a body that would not exist in any other way. The Body of Christ is unique. All members of this Body are called to acknowledge the value of the other members. There is a rich diversity of membership that is appreciated by those who have Christ as the head and the Spirit as unifier. As the Body of Christ, the church is composed by several ministries, which cannot function alone and only properly function together. The identity of the church as the Body of Christ, and what this means for the life and ministry of the church—its nature and purpose—is located within the celebration of the Eucharist.

THE EUCHARISTIC CHURCH

The Eucharist makes the church. The form and content of the Eucharist is the basis and model for the form and content of the church. Put another way, the Eucharistic Body of Christ as the ecclesial Body of Christ exists as a normative form and content recognizable in both. What follows is a description as well as a prescription; it is an account and an argument. We will explore the Eucharist in an effort to present an ecclesiology derived from, and expressive of, its liturgical form and theological content.

The liturgical form of the Eucharist is that set of actions that are its enactment.[6] These actions form an economy of performance. Therefore, we will take these actions in turn and address the question of the church in this way. Overall, the Eucharist is a ritual event; it is a prescribed action. The church is an event; it is a verb before it is a noun. We perform church as a celebration that happens in the fertile presence of God with the hope of a life given and renewed, shared and offered. This celebration of ecclesial life is a ritual. There is a way of performing it that permits the church to have its identity and vocation sustained over time and across place. This ritual is not a random set of actions and is not constantly re-created. Creativity is not a property of arranging or deciding what act will take place and in what order. Creativity is what the act allows to happen. The church abides through fidelity to normative actions.

The Eucharistic church is the gathering of the baptized. It is the presence of all its members gathered for a common purpose: we are here for the Eucharist; it is our primary reason for "being together." All of the baptized make the church what it is and not just one or two types of membership. Each way of membership, or role in the church's life, is referred to baptism for its essential meaning. One is what and who she or he is for the sake of the gathering of the baptized. The fullness of the church is a quality of baptismal representation. Gathering for a common purpose directs all other ecclesial actions and shapes its concerns and issues. Every deliberation and debate of whatever sort should be referred to the Eucharist for its direction and shape. This does not mean that all current and possible controversies can be settled by assigning them to some action or dimension of the Eucharist thus bringing clarity and resolution. What it does mean is that the church should not be divided up into disparate arenas of argument or to authorities not contingent upon the celebration of the Eucharist. Common purpose does not eliminate an array of objectives, but it does remove equal footing and a rigid hierarchy from among them.

The place of Scripture in the Eucharist is its place in the church. Scripture is not isolated from the life of the church, but it does speak to the church within its expectant hearing. The church does not gather without Scripture, but Scripture is not the purpose for gathering. What happens in the church belongs to the ecclesial imagination set forth by Scripture. In the celebration, Scriptural texts are not chosen by the participants but are presented by the church through a lectionary or cycle of readings. This lectionary takes the Eucharistic church through the great majority of Scripture and from all major sections of the canon: Pentateuch, prophets, wisdom literature, psalms, epistles, and concluding with the gospels. The whole of Scripture viewed through the prism of the gospels offers a vision to the church, which is to be Eucharistically realized.

Preaching within the Eucharist follows from the reading of Scripture. The proclaiming church has Scripture for its background and the communion of the baptized as its foreground. From the Scriptural narrative and vision, proclamation addresses a particular group of people with universal concerns. They are to hear what will be remembered by Eucharistic persons. Proclamation is not the only action of the church but is directed toward other actions. A proclaiming church will gather, confess, offer, share, praise, remember, invoke, and send. Proclaiming Scripture should make the church hunger and thirst for the body and blood of Christ.

When it occurs, the recitation of the Nicene Creed within the celebration of the Eucharist renews and rehearses the church's stewardship of the boundaries of its believing fellowship. The Eucharistic church maintains the parameters of the Christian faith; it knows the freedom of tradition. The Nicene Creed is not all the church believes or teaches, but it provides the outline for the responsible fulfillment of these tasks. The words of the Creed echo throughout the celebration, and the baptized are to hear them on their way to the altar as the story of communion.

The prayers of the people remind us that the church's life is always oriented toward God in prayer. The Eucharist is prayer, and the church cannot be the Body of Christ without standing in his place before the Father as the high priest who intercedes on behalf of the world. The church turns to God in every movement and action. It opens itself up both to the needs and conditions of the world as it opens itself to God. The church becomes that priestly place where heaven and earth meet, where fallen humanity comes to stand in the presence of the risen Christ. The Eucharistic church will not become complacent to the world and to God as long as it remains steadfast as a people at prayer. Throughout the Eucharist, the church acknowledges that what is to take place will do so as a divine action. The church exists as a witness that God acts in this world; there are a people gathered for this reason.

The confessing of sin, the pronouncement of absolution, and especially, the exchange of the Kiss of Peace, within the Eucharist, indicate that the church is a reconciled community. The common life of the baptized does not happen, is not realized, without being present together as those who are alienated from God, from each other, and from themselves. The church comes before God in the Eucharist with an acute awareness of the distance that only God's mercy can bridge. A church that cannot exchange the Peace is not living as it should, but this Peace stands between the separation of sinners and the communion of the Body of Christ. The peace of communion is known by the forgiven and the reconciled; those who have sought God's healing and heeded God's invitation in Christ. Hubris and self-confidence, reliance on ourselves, are not ecclesial attributes. The Eucharistic church is habitually seeking forgiveness for its human distortions of God's grace. A forgiven church is a peaceful one; the language of confession of sin prepares us for God's language of peace.

The Eucharist contains an offering and is an offering. Oblation is the pulse of the church's common life. Christ offers his life to the church, and the church offers itself to God in Christ. The church turns people into givers insofar as the church has a giving life. The Eucharistic oblation is a gift because it is offered out of desire for union and not as a coerced act. We offer gifts to God in response to God's gift to us, and we do so as seekers after God's life. The exchange of gifts is the economy of communion. Consequently, the church is to have a giving presence in the world; it will be known by its gifts. The Eucharistic church is giving life to world, and it will sacrifice for the sake of the life of others. It will not have the dominant profile of possessions but of gifts. What is the church offering the world, not what is the church taking from the world, becomes the question of mission.

The Eucharistic prayer begins with a dialogue, but not the usual kind. Often, dialogue is a way for two persons or a group to talk about themselves, and what they think and want. It is a way to get to know each other better, and possibly, to resolve differences or allow them to coexist. The cry for dialogue issues from the perception that if any progress is to made toward a possible human goal involving disparate persons or groups, then they need to talk to each other and see what agreement can be made. Eucharistic dialogue is not this kind of talk. The reason for entering into dialogue at the beginning of the Eucharistic prayer is so that everyone entering into it may be brought where it goes: "Lift up your hearts: we lift them to the Lord." This dialogue is not a negotiation among places held by interlocutors, but the displacement of selves in Christ: "The Lord be with you: and also with you." It is the beginning of a journey to where God would have us go. As the beginning of the Eucharistic prayer, the dialogue ushers us into the normative linguistic posture of the church: praise, thanksgiving, remembrance, invocation, and doxology. The language of the church is in a Eucharistic idiom. The deliberations, conversations, and dialogues of the church should regularly undergo a Eucharistic evaluation. Are we talking to each other in such a way that is leading us to where God would have us? Is this a dialogue for the sake of communion with God and with each other? Do we recognize the dynamics of praise and thanksgiving, of the remembrance of God's activity and the invocation for this action now, in our conversations?

The apex of the Eucharistic event is the reception of communion. The church is characterized by the reception of its life; it does not generate itself. The church exists as not only a witness to divine action but as the epiphany of divine life. It manifests what God's Trinitarian life looks like when shared with humanity. The distortion and depreciation of communion is a wound on the sacramentality of the church; its visible signification of, and participation in, the invisible life of God. In the Eucharistic economy, communion is given to everyone gathered in the same way. No matter one's role in the assembly, what one is or does, all receive the one and the same gift of communion. The common life of gift, the reception of the same Body of

Christ, is at the heart of the church's nature. Ultimately, we are all dependent on God in the same way. There is no one in the church who can exist without receiving this gift. We face each other from this reception, and we are forever accountable to it. Distinctions arise in how this life is lived and not within the life itself. The church is the shape God's gift of communion takes, but it does not have a life of its own.

The theological content of the Eucharistic church is the ecclesial extension of the presence and sacrifice of Christ within and as its common life. The reflections presented in the two previous chapters are brought to the question of the nature of the church. Christ is present in the Eucharist to those who are baptized into his death and life and to those who have gathered to meet him. Christ's presence is always to the church as well as an abiding within it. The church can never be completely and unequivocally identified as the presence of Christ: the church is not the same as Christ. The church is the Body of Christ as it gratefully responds and embodies Christ's address to it: "This is my Body." The ontology of the church is constituted by the sacramental reception of Christ's body and blood. Faith in his presence is what motivates the church to assemble. The fullness of Christ's presence is available to the church: his past, present, and future. The history of Christ is present as the schema of what divine action looks like when faithfully embodied in human existence. Is the church marked by this history, or does it strive to make its own history? Christ's presence is his contemporary life of resurrection and ascension. He arrives to the church from beyond the boundaries of time and place. The church cannot allow itself to be defined and confined by any moment of history or any place in the world. However, the church is to be fully present to every moment and to all places. Furthermore, as Christ's presence is never collapsed into the church, the church's life is never collapsed into the world. The offer of presence is not to be confused with a homogeneity of presence encompassing both church and world. The church remains faithful to the Eucharistic distinction between presence to and presence as. Christ is present to the church in the Eucharist with his future. The church stands under the promise of fulfillment and hopes for a future it cannot realize. The Eucharistic future is not an extension of the present but the advent of God's future. The horizon of the heavenly liturgy to which the church shares in its praise of God tells us that the future of the church has been determined already. The appropriate ecclesial temporal question is not what will our future be, but how do we live this ecclesial future now?

The church's dependency on the Eucharistic presence of Christ serves as the anamnetic charge to not forget the centrality of Christ for its nature and purpose: "For no one can lay any foundation other than the one that has been laid; that foundation is Jesus Christ" (1 Corinthians 3:11). The Eucharistic Christ makes the church. The church works effectively only in humility. As epiphany of Christ, the church undergoes the disciplines of fidelity and transparency. It abides faithfully with all the modes of Christ's presence: Scripture, sacraments, assembly of the baptized, and in the poor, needy, and dispossessed. It is faithful to all the epiphanies of Christ. However, the church's fidelity should not obscure or obviate Christ's presence. The faithful church will leave room for Christ to be seen and heard; it will have Eucharistic transparency. This means that the church should not rush to close every gap of understanding or to settle every unresolved issue. The epiphanic church is not an anxious one. It is willing to return again and again to the presence of Christ in the Eucharist for the illumination that will guide it.

In the celebration of the Eucharist, the church remembers, proclaims, and participates in the sacrifice of Christ. The church is the space opened by this sacrifice. Christ's death on the cross pronounced the finality of human existence in all its forms, and as such, a space is created for the unmediated act of God. The resurrection will not be tamed by any human effort to justify or explain it. The space opened up by the cross does not provide any ground on which to build an ecclesial edifice with human effort. Sacrifice marks the nature and purpose of the church. The church shares in Christ's redemptive work; it does not have its own work to accomplish. Likewise, the church operates sacrificially. It is always willing to give up something for the sake of its own salvation and the salvation of the world. It knows and confesses that the breaking of its body prepares it for the descent of the Holy Spirit; sacrifice makes possible the wholeness of Christ's Body.

As a space opened up by the sacrifice of Christ, the church is a place where sacrificial living makes sense. In a world where consumerist culture and economic growth become more and more the harbingers of progress and success, ecclesial living becomes a clearer counter sign of human existence. Living for the sake of others in order to live abundantly cannot be comprehended by a mindset intoxicated by the pursuit of wealth. How much sacrifice, if any, does the church require of itself and of its members? Is sacrifice taught and modeled? Also, the ecclesial Body of Christ will identify with all those people who are being sacrificed by the violence of power and the corruption of greed. From the Eucharistic economy, where Christ is "both victim and priest," the church will seek out all victims and offer them the life of communion. This is a tangible life of food, drink, love, and a place to belong. The Eucharistic church is the place where victims are gifts, and sacrifices can be redeemed. The church as the Body of Christ will not identify with the perpetrators of violence or the marketeers of greed. The Eucharistic church will not be counted among the soldiers taking Christ to the cross nor among the money changers in the temple that Christ will need to drive out.

ONE, HOLY, CATHOLIC, AND APOSTOLIC

The four traditional marks, notes, or characteristics of the church are that it is one, holy, catholic, and apostolic. Each of these terms could receive its own theological treatment and then be applied to the church. However, an appropriate theological understanding of each of them will be done with the church in mind. That is, these are dimensions of the totality of ecclesial reality and not autonomous categories of thought. As theological dimensions, they are not located solely within the institutional limits of the church but are always ultimately and primarily referred to God. The relationship between God and the church, as has been argued, is one of communion. This communion is established in Christ and by the Holy Spirit principally and paradigmatically in and through the celebration of the Eucharist. The Eucharist makes the church. How then are we to account for the oneness, holiness, catholicity, and apostolicity of the church? Each of these notes will be investigated according to the nature and purpose of the Eucharistic church presented above.

Ecclesiology in the twentieth century had an abiding interest in ecumenism. The unity of the church or churches was a question that attracted a variety of answers. Through monographs and several ecumenical dialogues the oneness of the church proved to be an elusive goal. How elusive depends on a working definition of the goal of unity. Is unity an attribute more of the visible or of the invisible church? Is unity a uniform church resulting from the organic consolidation of the churches? A recurring reference of ecumenical dialogue or movement is Jesus' high priestly prayer that his disciples be one as he and the Father are one (John 17). This prayer is not that the followers be one in any way they see fit, or that they adopt whatever idea of unity is regnant at the time. Jesus prayed that the church be one as he and the Father are one; the church is called to share the unity that exists between Jesus and his Father.

We can speak of three basic types of unity; one is directly related to the Eucharist, while the other two are implicated. One type is substantial unity. All are one because they share the same substance. There is a basic reality or inner substance that is identical across its many existences or representations. For the churches to be one in this way, we would need to either recognize the same substance found in all of them or establish this sameness. Again, this would depend on whether our accountable reference is the visible or invisible life of the church, the institutional or the mystical. Regardless, unity resides in sameness.

Another approach to unity is through a common will rather than a common substance. The churches are one because they all do the same thing, or they do something together. We could identify an action or ministry that belongs already to all of the churches, e.g. baptism in the name of the Trinity or proclamation of the Gospel. On the other hand, we could look for ways for the churches to do something together, e.g., projects of service or mission. Unity can be realized through a common or cooperative action. The first type of unity involves the nature of the church and the second the will.

The third type of unity implicates both nature and will while redefining them. Unity can be conceived as the mutuality of the giving and receiving of selves. Two or more selves completely give themselves to the other and receive the other's gift of self. This mutuality is total, such that the selves are unified or in unity with, in, and for each other. Here we have the unity that does not arrange preexisting lives into a putative commonality nor argue for a prior sameness. Oneness is a sacrificial reality. Of course, this is the unity of divine communion, even though we still use the language of a same substance and will. However, we properly conceive of substance and will, nature and act, in terms of communion as the mutuality of giving and receiving. Where this type of unity becomes less abstract and more concrete is in the celebration of the Eucharist. The unity that exists between Jesus and his Father was apophatically manifested on the cross and renewed in the resurrection. Jesus' cry, "My God, my

God, why have you forsaken me," did not occlude his relational gift to the Father: "into your hands I commend my spirit."

Ecumenical dialogues among several churches have led to statements of agreement about the Eucharist, often focused on the questions of presence and sacrifice. Some of these agreements are called "substantial." Yet, not all churches share the communion of the Eucharist; they do not give and receive the Body of Christ from each other. Various theological rationales are put forward for this state of affairs, principally focused on either doctrinal differences or nonrecognition of ordained ministries. Different churches approach the Eucharist from their theological and ecclesiological differences. The Eucharist is a goal pursued by other means. What is missing is that sacrificial act of communion: "into your hands I commend my spirit." The Eucharistic church would pursue unity from within its already practiced economy of giving and receiving of selves; unity is deepened and expanded and not achieved. The authoritative frame of reference for Christian unity would be the given and common celebration of the Eucharist, and how everything else does or does not make ecumenical sense within its scope. We would no longer have an ecumenical approach to the Eucharist but a Eucharistic approach to ecumenism.

The holiness of the church is a divine property. The church is holy through its participation in the life of God. The Eucharist makes the church holy by setting it apart for God's purpose through sanctification and transformation. The church gathers from the world to stand in the presence of God. The church inhabits the Eucharistic place expectantly, to hear God's Word, to receive forgiveness, to have the Holy Spirit poured over it, and to be taken into Christ's communion. The church goes to the Eucharist to be changed and to be transformed. A sign of the church's holiness is its willingness to turn toward God in thanksgiving and petition, in praise and invocation. It recognizes its dependency on God and practices it in all of its activities. How comprehensively is the life of the church one of prayer? Since holiness is never achieved by human effort, an overly busy church can become preoccupied with its own doings and not contemplate the presence and action of God to and on itself. The Eucharist is the church's preparatory act for God's transformative act. It is a reminder both that the church is called to be holy, and of how holiness is given and manifested.

As the event of God's bestowal of holiness on the ecclesial Body of Christ, holiness is an attribute of all the baptized; every baptismal life and vocation is a consecrated one. There are no institutional categories of holiness nor any prescribed gradients or degrees of holiness. The holiness of the church is meant to be lived and reflected by all of its Eucharistic people. Holiness is not a status within the Body of Christ but a witness to its character. This means that no one in the church, nor any part of the church, is relieved of the call to holiness. There are no surrogate holy people or places within the church. The holiness of the church radiates from God's sanctifying presence lived by the whole church.

The catholicity of the church is rooted in the local celebration of the Eucharist.[7] As the Eucharist, the wholeness of the church is represented and enacted. If the Eucharist makes the church, then each Eucharistic celebration makes the church in that particular place. The Eucharist presents both the formative focus and the visionary scope of catholicity. The first use of the term "catholic" for the church was in the early second century by Ignatius of Antioch, "Wherever the bishop appears, let there the multitude of the people be, just as wherever Jesus Christ is, there is the catholic church."[8] The bishop presides over the celebration of the Eucharist in which the body and blood of Jesus Christ is present and received by the whole church gathered in one place. The wholeness of the church, its catholicity, is constituted by this gathering around Christ. The fullness of Christ's presence to the church, and its gathering to meet him, is the formative focus of catholicity. The bishop's presence is the focal point of gathering for the Eucharist, for there is no gathering of this kind without him. The catholicity of the church is rooted in the local Eucharist and branches out from there. This means that catholicity is not a universal and abstract principle hovering over the church but is a quality of the common life of the Body of Christ.

The catholicity of the Eucharistic church manifests a vision of a renewed humanity. The new humanity in Christ is a transcendent reality. The differences existing among humanity are not occasions for fragmentation nor for elimination. In the Eucharistic gathering of the church, diversity is the necessary condition for catholic transcendence. The primitive gathering of the whole church with the bishop, and around the presence of Christ in the Eucharist, was of all the baptized in one place or city. This is the practice behind Ignatius' statement. All Christians from a variety of economic, ethnic, and social places assembled around the one bishop at the one Eucharist for the one Christ. This type of gathering was unique and served as a witness to the catholicity of God in Christ and with the Spirit unbounded by the human conditions of difference. Each Eucharist then was an epiphany of what a redeemed humanity might look like and of how a catholic world would appear.

Of course, the reality and vision thus described does not for the most part exist in our contemporary churches. We might have many Eucharists taking place in one city spread across different churches. However, two points can still be made. First, the catholicity of the church is not only rooted in the local celebration, it is a sharing in the eschatology of the Eucharist. Every Eucharist is a sacrament of God's future in Christ when "all will be in all." The heavenly direction of our Eucharistic prayer—Christ is high priest for the whole church—reminds us that our differences are not meant for division, and that they are our sinful work and not God's redemptive act. Second, we can strive to avoid turning our celebrations of the Eucharists into liturgical chaplaincies to specific groups based on age, interests, views, or needs. The Eucharist is not one more demographic grid but the one Body of Christ with many members.

The Eucharistic church is apostolic because it exists as a succession of Eucharists through time with its ministry and teaching. Apostolicity is the ecclesial concern for its origins, succession, and continuity. The Eucharistic assembly is the origin of the church, of the *ecclesia*. Hence, the celebration of the Eucharist is the reiteration of the original church; it is a return to its apostolic origin. The church does not pursue its own originality away from the Eucharist and its inherent accountability. Any development of practice or teaching would be required first to make Eucharistic sense.

Apostolic succession is constituted by the handing on and receiving of Eucharistic ministry and teaching. Bishops are ordained for the sake of the Eucharist and its ministry. Bishops ordain priests and deacons within the context of the celebration of the Eucharist with the church present for the reception of Christ's body and blood as an act of communion. That is, the ultimate reason for the gathering is not the ordination of someone; this is done on the way to communion. The apostolic church is faithful to its ultimate purpose for gathering, while being stewards of what is required for the succession of Eucharists. The Eucharistic church leads a successive life, one that will continue wherever the ecclesial Body of Christ renews its origin.

The continuity of the church can be maintained by a variety of means. Its teachings and practices can perdure through time as they are kept and performed. At times this continuity can be fragile or threatened by what appears as an innovation or distortion. In these cases, discipline can be imposed to maintain the continuity, or continuity can be reassessed in such a way that the new thought or practice is incorporated. The crucial question is what is the basis for authentic and faithful continuity of the church? Perhaps not every idea or act is essential to the church's apostolicity as a recognizable continuity among generations of Christians. To pose the question of continuity from the Eucharist, or as the Eucharist, is to view continuity as the endurance of the visible manifestation of the Eucharistic economy of faithful action and attendant teaching. What has continued in the Eucharistic celebration will continue to do so. This is the apostolic vocation of the Eucharistic church.

CHAPTER 5

LIFE

I am the living bread that came down from heaven. Whoever eats this bread will live forever; and the bread that I will give for the life of the world is my flesh.

John 6:51

The Eucharist is a way of life. It is not a self-enclosed event that we visit for purposes originating outside of itself. Even though we often do go to the Eucharist for a host of reasons identified within our non-Eucharistic life, the Eucharist is a place to learn the reasons and ways of the "host." The Eucharist is not just an object of thought and understanding, and not a resource for help with the different vicissitudes of life. It is the manifestation and formation of what life looks like in the presence of God, of who we are as baptized people, and of how to act toward the reception of the gift of Christ's communion. The Eucharist is how communion with God and with each other in Christ and the Spirit appears in a place and time. The Eucharist is the epiphany of communion with all of its demands. It is where and how we learn to live.

Life has many facets or dimensions; so much so that our experience can be one of fragmentation and confusion. We cannot make sense of the whole of our life because we have no place to start and no overarching principle to arrange all the parts into a coherent whole. We can live as life comes and not have an intentional and purposeful life. It is easy to become awash and overwhelmed by the needs and wants of the moment, either ours or someone else's. An individualism can set in whereby we are constantly deciding what is best for me, or what do I want, or how do I feel, how do I think, and what do I want to do? Exhilaration, boredom, and anxiety characterize the individual self and its putative freedom. What about the Eucharistic self?

The Eucharistic life is shaped by our reception of gift; it is more received than constructed. It is a creative life because it creates life and is not a life that creates. The Eucharist bestows freedom for and as communion. Within the celebration of the Eucharist, we learn all of the dimensions of the Eucharistic life. We are offered, and we are invited to inhabit, an imagination of humanity being restored and renewed by participation in the vision and will of God. The kind of life that Jesus came to give for the life of the world is faithfully enacted in the Eucharistic celebration. However, this life is not limited by the celebration but is to overflow its ritual boundaries and become the rite of the new humanity.

The economy of the Eucharist, the way it works, provides the structure and dynamic for the Eucharistic life. The progression of actions that form the Eucharistic event become the dimensions of life, the how and way we act from it. This exploration of the Eucharistic life will proceed through each of the constitutive actions. A reflection on the action as one of the Eucharistic event will be developed as an action and dimension of the Eucharistic life. We will move from the liturgy to life. We will attend to the economy of the Eucharist; how each action makes sense in light of the other actions. It should be noted that I am speaking of actions and not parts. The Eucharist is a verb before it is a noun. Its performance is not a product of the mind but a commitment of the will. The actions of the Eucharistic economy are: gathering, listening to Scripture, confessing a common faith, praying for others, confessing sin, receiving forgiveness, sharing the peace of Christ, offering, remembering Jesus, living by the Spirit, and receiving communion.

GATHERING

The first act of the Eucharist is gathering. Reflection on what it means to gather, what is involved in gathering, for the Eucharist, will set the tone for consideration of all the subsequent actions. There is something fundamentally at stake, a basic prior commitment, in gathering for the Eucharist. Are we willing to be gathered, are we committed to how being a Christian, a member of the church, the Body of Christ, displaces us from our self-styled and autonomous places. Are we willing to enter a foreign land in order to come home?

Are we willing to sacrifice the home we own for the one we can only inherit?

Before engaging these questions, and how they open up for us the true nature of the Christian life, the Eucharistic life, we need to train our imaginations for what lies ahead. We need to nurture the imaginative place into which we are being gathered. What are the images of life that guide and challenge us? What do our desires look like when we add pictures? Maybe, our issue is not learning a new imaginative world but having one at all. In this age of bloated information and "reality" entertainment, we easily fall into the habit of paying others to imagine for us, or we become voyeurs of others' imagination. One trait of the Eucharistic life is a strong imagination, and not one borrowed from the professionals of the age, but one nurtured by the great tradition of imagination. What does the kingdom of God look like? What does a holy life show us? What images present themselves to those people who say over and over again "heaven and earth are full of your glory?"

Let us begin to imagine what it means to be gathered with this image:

> But you have come to Mount Zion and to the city of the living God, the heavenly Jerusalem, and to innumerable angels in festal gathering, and to the assembly of the firstborn who are enrolled in heaven, and to God the judge of all, and to the spirits of the righteous made perfect, and to Jesus, the mediator of a new covenant. (Hebrews 12:22–24a)

When we come to the Eucharist, we tend to focus on ourselves, on our thoughts and feelings, the practicalities of getting there, even on how we look. And we bring these self-absorbed thoughts to the Eucharist itself; what we like or do not like about the liturgy, the sermon, the priest or minister, or the person in front of us. What is going on in the Eucharist is what is going on in us. This is not the imagination of the Eucharistic life.

Gathering for worship is essentially a passive reality. Fundamentally, we gather not for what we can do but what can be done to and for us. Also, we can speak of being gathered, the gathering itself is through an agency not of ourselves. Gathering and being gathered is to enter into the posture of openness and the sensibility of receptivity. We move into the time and space of gift and not possession, of receiving and not taking. We go to beg and not to buy.

Gathering is the dynamic of the church because it is the dynamic of salvation. Being saved is being gathered into God's presence and life, participating in God's life of communion. The church gathers because the church is gathering, and the essential act of this gathering is worship of the gathering God: Father, Son, and Holy Spirit. As such, we can speak of four dimensions of this gathering as church for the Eucharist: gathering *into*, gathering *with*, gathering *for*, and gathered *by*.

In the Eucharist, we gather into the company of those who have gathered faithfully since the first celebration of the Eucharist. We are gathering into the church through time and across time. We are brought into the great tradition of the Eucharistic church and into the company of all gathering Christians. We are gathered into a common life and common faith, into Christ and into God. We inhabit a life with common actions (basic acts of the Eucharist) and a common story (Scripture).

We gather with other baptized persons. The Christian and Eucharistic life is not an individual pursuit; its fullest and normative expression is a company of persons, not the solitary soul, but the communion of saints. It is this "with" that constitutes our identity. The Father identifies with Jesus, Jesus with the Father, Jesus with us, we with Jesus in our baptism. The Eucharistic identity is not an isolated character within, but the reality created by our being identified with Christ, Christ being identified with us, and our being identified with each other in and as the Body of Christ. We gather with all Christians who are gathering for the arrival of the risen Christ in the midst of their various celebrations of the Eucharist. We gather with the heavenly assembly: "angels, archangels, and all the company of heaven."

When we gather for the Eucharist, what are we being gathered for? The question of purpose is asked in the passive voice: What purpose will be manifested or revealed? We can have an initial intention for going to the Eucharist, and we can have many well-defined and ambiguous reasons for going. Whatever is the state of our intent or resolve, essentially we go as an act of fidelity, to enter the place of discovery. This means that we should not look to the Eucharist with a clear sense of purpose or with a specific goal in mind. We go for God's purposes. The purpose of gathering is juxtaposed with an apophatic sensibility on our part. Gathering is the beginning of communion. Theologically and economically, we gather to receive God's life of communion through the gift of Jesus by the outpouring of the Holy Spirit. We gather to be reconciled with God, with each other, to receive the forgiveness of sins, to pray for others and for the world, to listen to Scripture, to share the peace of Christ, and to remember Jesus. We gather for the arrival of Jesus, who offers us his life of communion for the life of the world. We are gathered by the Holy Spirit.

What is gathered? The short answer is everything. The whole of life is what is meant to be gathered. There is not a non-Eucharistic area of life; we are not to leave anything or any part (dimension) of ourselves behind. Each dimension of the Eucharistic economy has a corresponding dimension to human living, all of which is destined for offering and for consecration. Therefore, as each dimension of the Eucharistic life is considered, the corresponding dimension of human life will be brought into the exposition of transformation.

LISTENING TO SCRIPTURE

After the baptized have gathered for the Eucharist, they listen to Scripture. It is significant that prior to any action by the people, they hear words conveying the actions, stories, and events of others within the scope of the relationship between God and God's people. There is a narrative of gathering that precedes this event to which listening is required. A narrative is presented that comes from the outside; it is not a story concocted for the moment by the assembly. They are to attend to the presence of a narrative that asks questions of them. That is, listening to Scripture within the Eucharistic economy is not an exercise in deciphering the text to find something useful. The fundamental posture is receptivity; we are listening expectantly. We are not to come to the Eucharist with a well-honed tale of who we are, and what we need. We listen to enter into the theological imagination that discloses who we are, and what we need or even desire.

Scripture is the common memory of the baptized. The memorial injunction of "Do this in remembrance of me" incorporates all memory of God, the whole remembrance of the meta-narrative of communion. As common memory, Scripture shapes, sustains, and renews our identity as a people made for Eucharist. The Eucharist is a gathering of several individual histories and memories ordered toward finding their transformative place in the common memory and history Scripture provides. We do not abandon our memories and histories. Instead, we offer them for the sake of a communion among them, for what and who transcends them. Listening to our common memory prepares us to confess a common faith.

CONFESSING A COMMON FAITH

The Nicene Creed began to appear in the celebration of the Eucharist in the East in the sixth century and gradually later became authorized in the West. While not said at every celebration, the Nicene Creed is a dimension of the Eucharistic economy both as it is and as it signifies the place of common faith. We will explore what saying this Creed means for the Eucharistic life and not what is said. Although the content is important, we will focus on the act of confessing a common faith.

Two types of confession characterize the Eucharistic life. The first type is associated with the recitation of the Nicene Creed, and the second type is associated with the confession of sins and will be discussed below. One type of confession is the act of adhering to a statement or set of beliefs preceding the confessors. There are statements of belief, truth, and meaning that one recites as a way of submitting to them. Confession is not a sharing of opinion, and the corporate act of confession is not an aggregate of opinion. In fact, agreement with content is not the essence of the confession; it is not an expression of what we think. It is to submit to the boundaries of belief so that one might learn to live in this new territory. The content becomes the subject of thought; we are to wrestle with what is said. The Creed, and whole Eucharist, is the way that we are incorporated into the mind of Christ, which exists as the ecclesial Body of Christ. The development of Creeds began in a Christian *regula fidei*, a rule or a way to regulate the faith. Faith as that which is believed, in contrast to faith by which one believes, is not an amorphous entity requiring our agreement to keep it afloat. Faith is a regulation of Christian life; it keeps us heading the right way. The recitation of the Nicene Creed in the Eucharist is directed forward and is not a bit of nostalgia for the old days of certainty. The Creed is our way to communion.

Intercommunion among churches is a vexing topic posed by the relationship between common faith and Eucharistic communion. At what stage of common faith do churches share communion with each other? Many churches do this now, but some do not. Similarly, a church might deny communion to its members because they do not agree with some aspect of the church's teaching, or common faith.

Are there distinctions among teachings so that some pertain more directly to communion than others?

The common faith recited and received in the Eucharist requires commitment but not consensus. A theme present in each dimension of the Eucharistic life is that communion is received by the offering self, the offering assembly, and is not an achievement of proper order and thought. We do not achieve, possess, or produce communion, but we do submit faithfully to its life and demands. Confessing a common faith is a visible manifestation of a gathering of persons for the purpose of sharing a life given to them. These gathered, confessing, persons will keep meeting each other within this faithful act, a place to encounter confessors from previous ages and other Eucharistic celebrations within this common faith.

PRAYERS OF THE PEOPLE

As evidenced in Justin Martyr's outline of the Eucharist from the second century, an abiding basic action has been prayers offered for the church, the world, and all those in need. It was the practice of the early church that the newly baptized were brought into the Eucharist to join the assembly for these prayers. This action is the priestly prayer of all the baptized; their intercession for others before God. These prayers indicate two dimensions of the Eucharist and of the Eucharistic life: praying for others and prayer itself.

The entire Eucharist is an act of prayer. The baptized are gathered for various types of prayer, but most of all for prayer itself. As prayer, as an act of praying, the Eucharist is a time to practice the disciplines of drawing near to God, or of allowing God to be present to us. One of the great obstacles to prayer is distraction, and we can easily become distracted by liturgical details and either our performance or view of them. Also, we can be distracted by our lack of preparedness for these details; we can be anxious or apathetic. What is missing either by perfectionism or incompetence is transcendence. The details of the liturgy become ends and not means; they can form a matrix of personal assessment. We master the details, the basic movements and texts, so that they can locate us before God in prayer where we can stand on the edge between the visible and the invisible, between immanence and transcendence. Obsession over the liturgical minutiae put us in the midst of human concern and not on the brink of God's expectant agency. Praying the liturgy is integral to action and knowledge, and to practice and theology. Praying the Eucharist is to be moved along by its economy, and to be taken where it is going.

In whatever form they have existed in the tradition, both Eastern and Western, the prayers of the people, the intercessions, give voice and intent to a vision of God acting at the limits of human capacity. We intercede for those who are in need, who are weak, who, above all, unambiguously require God's agency in their lives. The intercessions permit the perception that human effort does not always yield success, or that life can exceed the grasp of human control. There is a recognition that our world and church stand before God as prayer and as a petition for divine mercy. This dimension of the Eucharist and of its life brings the church and the world to the same place of pleading. The difference is that the church pleads for itself and for others; it directly calls on God to fulfill and renew its life, while the world is brought into the movement of intercession by the church.

The priestly prayers of the baptized break open our human tendency to not venture beyond our own lives. These intercessory prayers are a nexus of transcendence: beyond our own concerns in particular and beyond all of humanity in general. By the transcendence of ourselves into an awareness of the needs, desires, and frailty of others, we open ourselves to the transcendence of God, to what lives beyond ourselves. The presence of others' need for divine mercy can teach us the presence of our need for the same mercy. This is one way that the catholicity of prayer is lived and renewed. The Eucharistic life shares the catholic vision of God's action on the whole of life, the whole church, and on the whole world. We are not made whole by God until we stand to pray for ourselves and others within the event of communion.

CONFESSING SIN

The confession of sin has been an act within the Eucharist or preparation for it. Within the Eucharist, this confession is general and public, while outside of the Eucharist, it is particular in form and private. The relationship between confession of sin and Eucharistic celebration touches upon two fundamental theological categories: anthropology and soteriology. We cannot consider these categories exhaustively, but certain aspects of them are salient to an outline of the Eucharistic life.

In the above discussion, the confession of faith was explored as the movement of the self from without to within: the adherence of persons and communities to a set of beliefs and to the boundaries of a common faith. The confession of sin is the inverse movement: from within to without. It is the expression of our interior life; it is an attempt to articulate who we really are as known only by the self and by God. This act of confession is an exercise in discernment; it is the effort to engage the honest self. Honesty is difficult work. We have layers of rationalizations, self-serving perceptions, and habits of skewed thinking. Honesty about ourselves cannot be attained by a self-willed and more intense psychological focus on our interior lives. We require a counternarrative and a schema of accountable actions. We are formed for honesty; we learn what honesty looks like when we allow questions of life to be put to us: Who are you, what are you, and why are you here? We are able to answer these questions as we are formed by the habitual actions of the Eucharist and not by the recurring patterns in our heads and in our own habits. Honest selves are seeking communion.

The confession of sin brings an awareness that one is a sinner. However we might delineate and define sin and sins, this confession is an utterance of disorder, of some negative aspect or reality of our life. Furthermore, the movement of this awareness of sin from within to without declares that we are in need of an action beyond ourselves. Confessing sin is not the same as noticing you have a few problems on which you should work. It is not asking for help with some personal projects. Confessing sin is saying you are a sinner who requires the redemptive act of God in order for you to become yourself in Christ. This is an act of baptismal honesty directed toward the Eucharistic life.

When confession of sins is an act of the whole assembly, a general confession, the individual experiences the added dimension of appearing before and with others as a sinner. This is the act of being honest with each other; it is how we express our corporate identity as sinners. There can be no hiding our weaknesses and vulnerabilities from each other. The Eucharistic life fosters relationships of honesty and risk, the lack of pretending to be otherwise, of hiding behind what we might consider our "best face," which actually hides the face of Christ from each other. Every assembly of Eucharistic Christians must have its moment of corporate confession, of acute awareness that left to our own will and nature, we will not inhabit the communion God offers. Confession is laying bare the futility of isolated human behavior, the stripping away of the pretense that we can achieve what we are "supposed" to do, or what we "can" do, or even what is the "right" thing to do. Without the presumption of being a sinner, both in a personal and corporate sense, we will not desire God's communion. Instead, we will be tempted to maintain a dimension of control, dignity, and ownership. We will not have reconciliation but negotiation.

RECEIVING FORGIVENESS

How we come close to God, how we desire intimacy with God, and how we begin seeking life with God is foundational to what will take place. There is a chasm of grand theological proportions between coming before God with the desire for God's unique and exclusive act on us and asking God to act in useful and helpful ways. God is not a three-person support group. The Eucharist is not an event of mutual encouragement, and is not one more enlightened human effort at community building. The forgiveness of sins comes from outside of us; it is an act untainted by the human pretense of achievement. We get closer to the reality of communion as forgiven sinners, those in whom God is initiating change.

Being forgiven is knowing that we can start fresh with God. Our personal and corporate histories are only decisive when we do not confess them and make them an offering to God. Asking for forgiveness is emptying the tomb; receiving forgiveness is God's unbinding and letting us go. Where does one go when they have been forgiven, when their history is made by God? "O send out your light and your truth; let them lead me; let them bring me to your holy hill and to your dwelling. Then I will go to the altar of God" (Psalm 43:3–4a).

We receive the forgiveness of sins. The posture for forgiveness, for God's act, is receptivity. God bestows forgiveness on receptive selves, those who are ready to transcend their own limits, natures, wills, and self-images. Forgiven sinners are bound to the forgiver and are called to see themselves and each other in the forgiver's illumination and perception. What happens is not a cleaning of the old self; it is the renewal of the baptismal self and of the Eucharistic vocation to communion.

So if you have been raised with Christ, seek the things that are above, where Christ is, seated at the right hand of God. Set your minds on things that are above, not on things that are on earth, for you have died, and your life is hidden with Christ in God. When Christ who is your life is revealed, then you also will be revealed with him in glory. (Colossians 3:1–4)

Who we "really" are will be shown to us in the revelation of Christ: to know ourselves is to know him. The Eucharist is the event when the baptized come out of hiding. Christ's presence in the Eucharist, present to us and present as us, offers a perception that abandons our customary coordinates for evaluating ourselves and each other. Receiving the forgiveness of sins ushers us into the place where the human point of view is sacrificed. In order to appreciate this sacrifice, we need to reflect a moment on what constitutes a human point of view.

Are we in the habit of regarding ourselves and others from a human point of view? After all, is that not the only kind of view we can have? The human point of view is the perspective of the here and now. What captures our attention are the circumstances, concerns, and issues of the present. We can fixate on what is the case now, on our thoughts and emotions, on all that forms what life is like today. On a grander scale, we dismiss anything as truthful or knowable if it cannot be grasped and understood by the pure powers of human reason or by the undeniability of personal or cultural experience. If something cannot be known as a referent of human reality, then it either cannot be known or it does not exist. If a possible action will not serve immediately the progress of humanity toward fulfillment of any sort, then it should not be done. This human point of view reached its zenith in the modern age. We have experienced the glorious achievements of human thought and actions, and we have seen the evil that comes from humans left to their own devices.

What about our relationships with others? From a human point of view, we relate to others in terms of ourselves: who and what makes me happy and fulfilled or not. These relationships are limited inherently by those who enter into them. After all, we are only human. What is possible is what I can achieve, or what I am willing to do. Likewise, the other person is limited by her or his nature and will. One can only expect so much from ourselves and from others. From a human point of view, we can only act and think within our limits as humans, we can only relate as humans. All relationships are bound by the humans that enter into them. Nothing can be expected that is not possible for me or for the other person, from a human point of view.

> From now on, therefore, we regard no one from a human point of view; even though we once knew Christ from a human point of view, we know him no longer in that way. So if anyone is in Christ, there is a new creation: everything old has passed away; see, everything has become new! All this is from God, who reconciled us to himself through Christ, and has given us a ministry of reconciliation; that is, in Christ God was reconciling the world to himself, not counting their trespasses against them, and entrusting the message of reconciliation to us. (2 Corinthians 5:16–19)

In Christ, God has brought something new into the world, into human nature and will. This newness is the life of God that God offers to share with us. Yet, how can we share the life of God when we are not God? How can we overcome our limits as humans, breaking out of our nature and actions? How can we relate to God from a human point of view? Simply put, we cannot. Instead, God comes to us in Christ to reconcile us to God, to bring us into the unifying life of God, the life of eternal loving communion between the Father, the Son, and the Holy Spirit. It is God's nature and life not to be limited by individuals negotiating their relationships with each other. In the divine life, a broken relationship would be death.

When God's life enters into receptive human lives that are strained and distorted by broken relationships among each other and alienation within, God forgives sins and works reconciliation. God does not sit still accepting our intransigence and self-justifications about what is wrong with ourselves and with others. God's presence is always a movement from and toward others. This is why God's presence in Christ is always the presence of, and for, reconciliation. There is no genuine Christian life, no Eucharistic life, without reconciliation. Belonging to Christ in baptism is to have God's point of view, the Eucharistic vision of all people being reconciled to God and each other in Christ. Receiving the forgiveness of sins is the beginning of reconciliation, which is integral to the life of communion: the overcoming of separation and alienation. Reconciliation happens when we sacrifice the human point of view, offer ourselves to meet each other in Christ, and become the new creation. One characteristic of this reconciled and Eucharistic life is sharing the peace of Christ.

SHARING THE PEACE OF CHRIST

One of the "new" features of the rites of Eucharistic celebration developed during the liturgical movement of the twentieth century was incorporation of the exchange of the Peace. This act had either completely disappeared from the liturgy over the centuries or had become something confined to the sanctuary performed by the ordained. Customarily known as the "Kiss of Peace" in the ancient church, this act was an important sign and demonstration of the type of life Christians shared in common. In the rites of several liturgical churches, the exchange of the Peace occurs prior to the offertory and Eucharistic prayer, while in the Roman Rite it is done just before receiving communion. Regardless of when it occurs, it is a sign that points to that communion.

What is this exchange of the Peace? Before addressing what it is, we should address what it is not. When introducing a liturgical act, or any "new" act for that matter, into the life of a church or congregation, there is a tendency to absorb it into a set of meanings that exist already. What people think, how they act, or who they are become the context of understanding. Unless the act is formative, it will be informative. That is, unless the theology and form of life to which this act speaks is taught, we will use it to speak in our own usual way. The act will inform us; it will be adapted to the form of life we have constructed for ourselves, or what everyone else seems to think and do. The Peace becomes a way to say hello, to catch up, or to engage in good willed chit-chat. The exchange of the Peace can be the occasion to speak to each other the way we do outside of the Eucharist, exterior to the Word and Spirit driven movement into divine communion.

I have entitled this dimension of the Eucharistic life "Sharing the Peace of Christ," because that is what we are called to do; this is what reconciled people do. First, let us consider the word "sharing" rather than "exchange," or as it is sometimes put, "greet." Sharing includes what takes place between two persons or within a group, but it also points beyond this transaction. We can say that two persons share something between them, and that they share in something beyond themselves. They share what does not belong to either one of them or to the group. This sharing is a further reflection and instantiation of what began with the confession of sins and continued in the reception of forgiveness: the economy of gift. The Eucharistic life is humanly instigated by the baptismal will to be a gift (confessing), receive a gift (forgiveness), and share a common gift (peace).

We do not share a generic or putative peace. We share the peace of Christ: "Peace I leave with you; my peace I give to you. I do not give to you as the world gives" (John 14:27). Christ is not endorsing a peace already at hand; he will not allow himself to be associated with a version of peace being promoted by individuals or groups of humanity. The divide between what he is offering and what the world or powers or politics might offer is firmly established and cannot be bridged even by the most enlightened and best intentions. Why is this? Because the peace that Christ is talking about does not exist without him, "For he is our peace" (Ephesians 2:14a). The presence of Christ's peace is his presence. This means that we cannot purchase the peace of Christ without being made anew in him. His peace is not gained by following his example; this is not an ethical worldview or set of values. Actually, his peace is known through the abandonment of our stratagems for what we might take to be good and right. Christ's peace is shared by forgiven sinners offering themselves as subjects of God's will and partakers of God's nature. Christ's peace happens in him and as him; it is the peace of communion he gives to, and shares with, us. The Eucharistic life is sharing the peace of Christ; it is the life that shares Christ's presence. It is the event of Christ's gift of self; and consequently, it is where and how we learn to give.

Christ's presence interrupts the world's ways of peace and conflict, of fear and joy. Christ's freedom to bring a word of peace to anywhere at anytime will unsettle, maybe threaten, how we are seeking to settle a conflict or live in fear. In fact, Christ is free to alter what we think is a conflict or not, or where our efforts and energies might be directed. What we take to be a conflict among persons might be rooted in a conflict with God, our own alienation from our true peace.

> When it was evening on that day, the first day of the week, and the doors of the house where the disciples had met were locked for fear of the Jews, Jesus came and stood among them and said, "Peace be with you." After he said this, he showed them his hands and his side. (John 20:19–20a)

Jesus enters a room filled with fear, and he enters as one who was not expected. Also, he enters a room that no one else could enter; the doors are locked from the inside. Jesus arrives in a situation structured to protect the inhabitants from anyone's arrival. To the locked in and fearful he says, "Peace be with you." He does not initiate a conversation with the disciples to ascertain how they are doing. He does not try to get a sense of the room. He declares a reality rather than conjuring one up or trying to persuade the disciples to feel differently. The simultaneity of this declaration with his arrival will not permit a separation between words, person, and reality. Jesus declares peace because he is a person of peace; he is the arrival of peace.

Jesus is a person of peace because he arrives from his relationship with the Father in the Spirit. He comes from peace and as peace. His identity is constituted elsewhere, from beyond the grave and all places of fear and conflict. He declares peace as one whose identity and worth are not being negotiated here. While in his earthly life he was going *to* the Father; in his risen life he is coming *from* the Father. However, he is not someone who has not known conflict, "he showed them his hands and his side." He has a history of violence that marks his arrival without being renewed or repeated. Jesus is not seeking vengeance, and he will not incite others to violence. Peace is not the absence of conflicted circumstances, situations, or events; peace is the absence of the conflicted self. Jesus arrives with a peace that breaks through and into the history of conflict and violence.

The Eucharistic life will experience conflict without being conflicted. Sharing the peace of Christ forms witnesses to this peace. Eucharistic persons will go where no one else will or can go and declare peace. The freedom of the forgiven allows them to trespass on the territories of conflict and fear. Eucharistic persons come from the gifted presence of Christ into the world. They arrive from the Eucharist having received a gift that the world cannot give. Being at peace, from peace, is the prerequisite state for witnessing to this peace. When Eucharistic people engage in "peace making," they can befall the temptations of world-giving peace. They can slip into the rhetoric and methods of resolving conflict that do not come from conversion in Christ, from his presence beyond the killing fields of human power. This is why ongoing faithful formation into the Eucharistic life through all of its dimensions is necessary. We need to cultivate our abiding receptivity to Christ's gift of peace if we are to enter locked rooms of fear with the unexpected declaration of peace.

OFFERING

The pivotal act between the "Liturgy of the Word" and the "Liturgy of the Table" is the offertory. As Justin Martyr's account revealed, this act of offering was part of the early church's celebration of the Eucharist. This was how the assembly moved toward, and prepared for, the Eucharistic prayer. What was offered was not money but food and animals, and this offering was distributed to those in need. You came to the Eucharist with something to offer; you came with a gift that made communion possible. Gifts were offered so that gifts could be received. The assembly was constituted by the exchange of gift and a common life was produced. Central to this action was the offering of bread and wine so that it would become the body and blood of Christ. This consecration happened only to *offered* bread and wine.

The offering that occurred in the Eucharist was not a solely cultic act; it was not confined to the liturgy. Offering for the sake of a common life was the way the church behaved.

> All who believed were together and had all things in common; they would sell their possessions and goods and distribute the proceeds to all, as any had need. Day by day, as they spent much time together in the temple, they broke bread at home and ate their food with glad and generous hearts, praising God and having the goodwill of all the people. (Acts 2:44–47a)

Why did these early Christians act this way? What would "possess" them that they would sell their possessions and share everything? Here indeed is the pivot point from seeking some aid or direction for one's life to seeking life itself. The Eucharistic life is not a gloss on a life centered in another place with a different set of normative behaviors and attitudes, or values. These Christians were inhabiting a new life and not trying to adapt the old life to a new idea. Their assembly was their neighborhood, their culture, and their nation. The question is not how does a good Jew, good Roman, good Greek, or good whatever act. The question is how does a person buried into Christ's death and resurrection act; how do we act as a Eucharistic people? One fundamental answer to this question is to behave like people whose life has been given to them from beyond the grave, from God in the risen Christ. This is sharing a common gift and not casting lots for a limited amount of resources.

For the most part, money defines our relationship to possessions. We buy things with money. We can or cannot own something depending on how much it costs. Our capacity to own or possess something is based upon what we have and how much is required: can I afford it? "What did that cost you?" "How much does it cost?" We ask such questions whenever we want to learn the value of something. If we know how much money it takes to have something, then we know if we can afford it or not. We ascertain the worth of something by its cost. Do we have enough money to own it? Those who own it must have the money. And, what does it say about the person who can afford it or not? Often, we take the worth of something as a sign of our own or someone's worth. In this way, we identify ourselves to others by possessions, by the cost of what we have. When we learn that a friend has bought something new, we are tempted to ask, "what did it cost?" By knowing the cost, we might gain some insight into our friend. Our friend becomes someone who can afford the cost of this new possession.

How much does the Eucharist cost? Nothing and everything. The Eucharist is not something we buy for ourselves; we cannot own it. The Eucharist is God's gift to us so that we might share God's life of communion. Jesus gave us the Eucharist, the way to share his life when the end of his earthly life was dawning. The Eucharist is the dawn of new life. Jesus died so that we might have the Eucharist. God can afford to buy the world through the Eucharist. The world is worth the Eucharist. We do not come to the Eucharist as those who decide whether we can afford to buy it. Instead, we come to make the sacrifice of praise and thanksgiving, we come to offer our desires for communion. The sacrifice of our lives: that is what the Eucharist costs. Stewardship begins at the altar. Eucharistic sacrifice is the basis for Christian stewardship.

THE PRAISE OF HEAVEN

The Eucharistic prayer begins with a dialogue between presider and people as an introduction to the first section of the prayer culminating in the Sanctus: "Holy, holy, holy Lord, God of power and might, heaven and earth are full of your glory. Hosanna in the highest." This text, drawn from Jewish liturgy (Isaiah 6:3), is found in all Eucharistic prayers beginning in the fourth century. The people join the oral presentation of the prayer in the Sanctus; it is one of the places where all voices are heard. In most liturgies, the Sanctus is preceded by the verse "joining our voices with angels, archangels, and all the company of heaven we sing." This is the moment when Eucharistic people sing the song of heaven.

Many fourth-century prayers are quite effusive in their evocation of heavenly worship leading to the Sanctus. There is a sense of standing before and within the heavenly place where true worship abounds. Giving voice to the heavenly realm opens up our perspective, our vision, as our mouths are opened. There is more here than just us; there is more going on than just what we do. Our language is not self-referential and not entirely expressive of ourselves. We offer our language to another sphere of meaning; we are not talking to ourselves. The abiding and normative addressee of the Eucharistic prayer is God the Father. The Eucharist is our relationship to God and is directed toward our place within God's full reality.

Given the horizon articulated by the Sanctus, the joining of heaven and earth, the Eucharist is never an earth-bound work. It is not performed in the idiom, or with the purpose, of community building, consciousness raising, good works motivation, or aesthetic safeguarding. The Eucharist is the invitation to become a heavenly being, one whose whole life becomes praise of God. This heavenly vocation does not excuse us from earthly concerns. On the contrary, as imbued with God's glory, earth is within the scope of divine action and care. Joining the heavenly chorus is sharing in the heavenly vision of all of creation as restored to its creator, as healed and reconciled, fed and clothed, and surrounded by fellow worshipers.

The Eucharistic life has a heavenly dimension. We are to practice the praise of God. Praising God is giving glory to God for no other reason or purpose than its performance: God is God. From the practice of praise, the habitual turning to God in doxology, we can awaken to ourselves as worshipers, those whose true selves and activity belong ultimately beyond ourselves. Praising and heavenly selves are dispossessed of earthly anxieties. How do I look, and how am I doing are quests abandoned at the altar of heaven. Other people are not competitors for life and truth but potential heavenly company, those who can share the Eucharistic loaf, the bread of heaven.

THANKSGIVING

Praise issues in thanksgiving. The Eucharistic prayer is often named "The Great Thanksgiving." Early on, as indicated in the prayers of the *Didache*, thanksgiving became a dominant and normative theme of table prayer. The Eucharistic life is a thankful life, one characterized by habitual thanksgiving. However, this thanksgiving stretches beyond the human exchange of appreciation. We give thanks for what has happened before us, to other people in different times and places. We give thanks for a history that is not available to us except through baptism and Eucharist. We are baptized into a history of thanksgiving, and we liturgically renew it by directly giving thanks for what did not happen directly to us. This is what it means to be thankful for salvation history. Through Eucharistic thanksgiving, if this is not too tautological, we do not make history so much as history makes us.

For what are we thankful? Often, we are thankful for getting what we want or desire. Our immediate sense of what would delight us, help us, or satisfy us sets the terms for a possible thanksgiving. Thanks is rendered when it is expected or even due. What about a giving of thanks for that which is initially unwelcome and unexpected; what about giving thanks for what we did not want? In this case, we might have to learn thanksgiving rather than it being a grateful reflex. We might be struck by an enticing thanksgiving for the strange and unplanned. In this way, thanksgiving is hopeful and prayerful. We give thanks not for what fills the gaps in our lives, but for what our life can become when taken into another life and its history. We *give* thanks for what *thanks* may give us.

We give thanks. The Eucharistic life is the communion of the thankful. A common life is acknowledged and realized by giving thanks for the same history and for the same action on everyone gathered. There is both a vertical and horizontal vector to this Eucharistic action. We reflected above on how thanksgiving transcends the self (vertical); but thanksgiving also binds selves to each other (horizontal). Entering into a common thankfulness can release us from a landscape partitioned by individual pursuits of interest normally traversed by efforts at influence. This is a time to see each other as givers of thanks and to be thankful for each other, to know ourselves within Christ's thankful place before the Father.

REMEMBERING JESUS

While offering is the pivotal move of the Eucharistic life, remembering Jesus is its center of gravity. Jesus' mandate, "Do this in remembrance of me," binds the Eucharistic action to the particularity of his person, and vice versa. We do not remember Jesus without Eucharist, and we do not have Eucharist without remembering him. This may sound obvious, but it is not always the case. We can pursue the meaning or relevancy of Jesus and of the Eucharist without ever making this a mutual and common effort. Our relationship to Jesus might be understood and nurtured in a variety of ways—academic, ethical, spiritual, or theological—without ever engaging the basic claims of Jesus' presence in the Eucharist, or how we are in communion with him in this normative event. We relate to Jesus, and he relates to us, as the Body of Christ. The Eucharist is our baptismal remembrance of the one to whom we belong. Remembering him is the renewal of our identity.

The "me" of this remembrance is the particularity with which we are to engage faithfully. This remembrance is not an exercise in keeping a distance from him, locating him in the alien past. It is the way to be present with him in his history and his presence in ours. Our own particularity becomes transformed, not forgotten, by this memorial mutuality. Remembering him as a particular person allows us to remember our own particularity without being defined by it. Sometimes we flee the details of life in a presumptive effort to draw an ideal picture of ourselves, or to forget who we really are. However, an abstract self is an unsaved self; it is not a Eucharistic self. Remembering Jesus is also characterized by vertical and horizontal movements. We are drawn toward his particularity through our own, and we are drawn to each other by remembrance of the same person. There is a communion of remembrance among those who do not hide nor hold their particular selves but allow them to be interwoven into one Body and one memory.

LIVING BY THE SPIRIT

A normative action of the Eucharistic prayer is the invocation of the Holy Spirit over the bread and wine, and often, over the people gathered (the consecratory and communion *epicleses*). Praise, thanksgiving, and remembrance coax the Eucharistic assembly to invocation: May the Holy Spirit come and realize among us what we have shared with heaven, with history, and with Jesus. The coming of the Holy Spirit relates what and who would remain separate if left to their own natures and histories. The Spirit releases things and people from their inherent destinies and bestows God's future upon them. The *epiclesis* is the invocation of the future that arrives from God's freedom.

Invokers of the Spirit are not under the illusion or delusion that they will accomplish what God desires for them. They know that singing the song of heaven, giving thanks for God's historical activity, and being centered in the memory of Jesus issues in the invitation to have this become their reality as well. The invocation of the Spirit is opening the gates of heaven and God's history so that this Eucharist may become the time and place where grace overflows the shores of the visible. Creatures are transformed into the Body of Christ and now have his destiny of communion.

The Eucharistic life progresses and matures through invocation of the Holy Spirit. There will be an abiding recognition that we cannot provide for our own future. What tangibly, visibly, and historically defines, or perhaps confines, us becomes that upon which the Spirit is invoked. The Eucharistic life is living *by* the Spirit, the agency that can never be mistaken as our own. As such, the domestication of the past or the present is a turning away from *epiclesis*. We must avoid getting stuck in our places of convenience, familiarity, and control. Eucharistic prayers conclude in doxology, in the eternal words of glory-giving, and this is where the Spirit takes us, within the future of God's communion.

COMMUNION

The economy of the Eucharist is a movement toward, and as, communion. Communion in the sense that all of the dimensions of the Eucharistic life are mutually present to, with, and in each other. There is a communion of dimensions, and there is a communion of life, a life of communion. The defining moment and act of the Eucharist is the reception of communion. Normally, we think of this moment as when the baptized come forward and receive the body and blood of Christ. This is true, but it is not an isolated truth; it is the truthful act of communion. We objectively receive communion for the sake of our subjectivity.

As reviewed above in the chapter on "Presence," a great deal of thought and argumentation has been proffered on the nature and extent to which the bread and wine become the body and blood of Christ. One side of debate stresses the objectivity of this change; the way in which the elements can no longer be just themselves, and how

Christ is *here*. The other side emphasizes the state of the receiving believer, the subjectivity of faith. Faith in the presence (objective): the presence of faith (subjective). Yet, when we employ the phrase "receive communion," we are already stretched beyond the facile dichotomy between object and subject, and even beyond presence and faith. The reality of communion is one of relational presence that does not permit divisions but rejoices in distinctions. Receiving communion is appropriately grasped as the symbiosis of two movements of presence.

The first movement is Christ into us. Christ makes himself available to our inner life. He is willing to enter the private places hidden from others, maybe hidden from ourselves. Christ's movement into us is a recapitulation of the vulnerability of the incarnation. He enters our flesh, while not being absorbed by it. He can be present to our vulnerability without being its victim. Here we have the Eucharistic Emmanuel: God with us. Christ is willing to be with us, within us, unto death. His Eucharistic reception parallels his own movement from incarnation through an earthly life culminating in the crucifixion. We receive Christ's body and blood into ourselves so that all we are can be found at his cross.

The second movement is we into Christ. The first movement is our reception of communion, and the second movement is our being received into God's communion as Christ's body. This second movement is primary; the first one is for the sake of the second. At every Eucharist, God the Trinity receives communion. We become Eucharistic gifts. This second movement into Christ and into God's communion parallels Christ's life from the resurrection through the ascension toward the second coming. The act of receiving communion is sharing in the resurrection, being displaced by the ascension, and awaiting the arrival of our full self. "Beloved, we are God's children now; what we will be has not yet been revealed. What we do know is this: when he is revealed, we will be like him, for we will see him as he is." (1 John 3:2)

The Eucharistic life is one of discovery. Through the kenotic offering of ourselves into Christ's life of communion, we discover who we really and truly are. This self revealed in Christ is both continuous and discontinuous with our created and historical self; it is the continuity and discontinuity revealed in the paschal mystery, between death on the cross and living from the Father. We should stay away from receiving communion, from going to the Eucharist, if we are unwilling to change, unable to move. "The Body of Christ: the bread of heaven. The Blood of Christ: the cup of salvation."

MISSION

The final act of the Eucharist is the dismissal of the people, the sending out of the Body of Christ into the world. While the Eucharist is the place and event of Christ's arriving presence with the offer of his life of communion, and the normative existence of the baptized, it is not the only place of God's action: "for the life of the *world*." However, our going out into the world on a mission is not to forget God's Eucharistic mission. We do not leave the celebration of the Eucharist motivated to do what we would have done anyway without the formation for mission enacted only by its celebration. There is a habitual temptation to fixate on our actions, on what we can do and the difference we can make. We might mimic other strategies of social change, other ways to influence and shape the world according to our vision of what is right. To paraphrase another saying: You can take a person out of the Eucharist, but you should not be able to take the Eucharist out of the person.

We are sent on the Eucharistic mission as those to whom Christ has been sent, and on whom the Holy Spirit has been sent. Our guides and coordinates for mission are derived from God's mission, from God's Eucharistic actions. There is a tendency to focus on our actions within the liturgy, on the propriety of our performance. The purpose of liturgical competency is transparency to divine action. Likewise, competency in mission allows for the epiphany of God's mission. Therefore, in order get our bearings for mission, we begin with the question, what is God doing in the Eucharist? What are God's Eucharistic actions?

We should keep in mind the principal of Trinitarian theology traced back to Augustine of Hippo, that the works of the Trinity outside of the Trinity are indivisible. We will thus survey God's Eucharistic behavior by not parceling out God's actions among the three persons. Instead, we can attend to the series of actions that constitute the dimensions of the Eucharistic life. God gathers the baptized. God speaks to us through the reading of Scripture. God has provided a framework for understanding who God is. During the prayers of the people, God listens to our needs and desires. In our confession of sins, God provides a place for honest reflection.

God forgives sins and grants a peace we can share with each other: God reconciles. In the offertory, God receives our gifts, what we are willing to offer of ourselves. In the Eucharistic prayer, God allows us to join the heavenly chorus, to return thanks for God's actions on our behalf, and to relate to the person and history of Jesus through memorial. God sends the Holy Spirit to realize what we cannot. God gives us the food and drink for which we have come. In the dismissal, God gives us a mission.

Our Eucharistic mission is the inhabiting and extension of God's actions from the Eucharist into the world. We are to gather people, and to allow them to be present to us as they are. We are to proclaim the Word of God to them, and to provide a basic and accessible framework for understanding who Christ is and why he matters for us, and possibly for them. Then, we are to listen to their needs and desires, allowing them to voice their own reality as petition. Listening to people in their own voice can lead to honest reflection and to an expression of a private disorder, a desire for help. Mission entails forgiveness; our unwillingness to allow past hostilities and divisions to chart our common future. We are to invite others to share the peace of Christ. This means being present amid conflict without being conflicted or conflicting. Mission is the joining together of disparate voices and languages into the heavenly praise of God. We are bound together by the abundance of all peoples and languages gathered before God's heavenly presence. Mission is giving thanks for God's history with other people beside ourselves, and for God's invitation to make this history one's own. The Eucharistic mission is teaching people how to remember Jesus in the midst of their own particularity. Mission is the invocation of the Holy Spirit over people. We know that the future God will provide for others is God's free action on them, and not the projection of our history and will. Mission is feeding people; it is giving life. This feeding is not just sustaining the minimum but preparing a banquet. We are not limited by the mathematics of need. We envision the joy of abundance. Finally, mission is forming missioners; sending out those to whom we have been sent. The abundance of the Eucharistic life overflows to the ends of the earth and to the end of the world.

CHAPTER 6

THEOLOGY

Our teaching is in harmony with the Eucharist, and the Eucharist confirms our teaching.[1]

Irenaeus of Lyon, Against Heresies, 4:18:5

The preceding chapters have been a sustained theological reflection on the basic categories entailed in the understanding and practice of the Eucharist. This reflection is to be guided by the Eucharist itself, by attending to its inherent economy. However, the scope of this endeavor is not confined directly within the liturgy and theology of the celebration of the Eucharist. There are broad implications for the nature and purpose of theology itself. That is, instead of just a theology of the Eucharist, we can and should delve into what the Eucharist of theology might involve. The following argument begins by posing the questions of the nature and method of theology. These questions will be pursued in a way that appreciates the current situation of theology, while arguing for the proper and foundational place for the Eucharist within any theological endeavor. Also, this reflection on the relationship between theology and the Eucharist provides a synthesis and a summary of the major themes developed above. I conclude with a proposal for a Eucharistic systematic theology. Therefore, one could say that I end this book on the Eucharist with an introduction to the Eucharist of theology.

THE SCOPE AND NATURE OF THEOLOGICAL QUESTIONS

What is theology, and how should it be done? These questions have never been answered easily because they entail various other questions and ultimate concerns. Theology can be approached from a myriad of perspectives, not least of which, are its origins and ends. Where does theology begin, with what does it begin, and what is the goal(s) of theology? In fact, it is fair to describe the current enterprise of theology as a pluralistic endeavor. There are many types or styles of theology, and not a few theologians would argue for the propriety of this pluralism. One account of the reason for the multiplicity of theologies attends to the diversity of those who do theology. Prior to the current state of theology, the variety of ecclesial confessions would be sufficient to render different theologies. There are different churches, confessions, and consequently, different theologies. The ecclesial context of the theologian would shape the theology produced. While this confessional and/or denominational multiplicity still should be appreciated, it no longer offers an adequate appraisal of our contemporary theological plurality. We also can note the changing contexts for the education of theologians, i.e., education in multidenominational institutional contexts with students and faculty representing a variety of confessions and primary interests. Also, theology studied within schools of religious studies associated with secular universities often accounts for a diversity reflecting the constructive efforts of individual theologians. The emphasis on "constructive" as opposed (perhaps not too strong a word) to "dogmatic" or even "systematic" theology does lead to the breakdown of confessional cohesion. Theologies can be classified not by confessional or ecclesial references but by normative paradigms or concerns, e.g., liberationist, feminist, or postliberal theology. One type or style of theology can be done by a collection of theologians drawn from several denominations. Instead of being a Methodist, Lutheran, or Presbyterian theologian, someone is more apt to self-designate him or herself as a postmodern, postliberal, or liberation theologian.

The existence of multiple theologies is due not only to different ecclesial confessions but to the differences among theologians. That is, different theologians construct different theologies. According to this perspective, what constitutes the self shapes ineluctably the theology done by the self. The modern self was viewed as having the potential for the objective exercise of pure reason. Theology should be a rational exercise whether one was reflecting on an objectively construed revelation or on the object of nature. Here, theology could be a science: the exercise of normative methodology engaging the object of study producing true knowledge. How we understand the self shapes how we understand theology. In a postmodern climate, we attend to the complexity and particularity of the self and to the multiplicity of selves. There is my-self and there are other-selves, and to understand the self one must maintain an abiding other-ness among all selves. There is no pure and universal self, and therefore, there can be no normative and universal theology. There are different theologies reflecting different theological-selves. Who I am means I will do theology differently than you will because of who you are. The complexities and differences among the selves are not arbitrary. These differences do not lie outside the self as choices to make. Difference is not just a matter of the will but is found first in the natural self. Difference is a priori as well as a posteriori.

This natural self, this nature, is not pure or universal. Nature is not an abstraction reached through speculative thought. Rather, nature is a product of history, culture, genetics, race, language, and sexuality. Therefore, one cannot speak of the self without employing these constructive realities. These terms and realities, and how they are understood within their representative disciplines of study, provide the spectrum on which to locate the self. We are born and develop within a place in the world, and we view the world from this place. We might say that having a place in the world does not allow someone to speak of, or understand, any other self existing in another place. Language and understanding belong to one place and not another place. Further reflection in this postmodern vein would move from different perspectives on one world rooted in the different selves to different worlds comprised of different peoples. This postmodern approach to the self takes up the modern anthropological starting point (the turn to the subject) and then deconstructs any notion of a pure, universal, or normative self.

The multiplicity within theology, or the various theologies, arises not just from the differences among those who do theology. This multiplicity reflects the different sources of theology. Certainly, the question of the sources of theology is shaped by the confessional context and by the theologian. What are the sources of theology? Is there one normative source from which one engages possible other sources? For many theologians, Scripture serves as such a normative source. For other theologians, religious experience, however understood, is the normative source that provides a way of interpreting Scripture or engaging tradition(s). A theological decision is made regarding the source, a decision about what will provide the normative content of theology. The decision of source shapes theological method.

That is, a theological method should be adequate to the source, and the source serves as the point-of-departure for a method. If the normative source of theology is Scripture, then a method would be employed that best serves to engage this source. The scriptural source would yield a scriptural methodology. Of course, there can be, and are, various ways to encounter Scripture as source, and various scriptural methodologies. The present point is the accountable relationship between source and methodology. Likewise, religious experience as theological source would yield a method appropriate to this reality. Therefore, the question of source involves the question of method, and indeed, all theological questions.

Questions regarding the sources of theology, and how theology identifies and addresses particular concerns, raises the deeper and abiding question of the purpose of theology. Why theology is done shapes how it is done. A multiplicity of purposes issues in a multiplicity of theologies. Is theology a way to understand ourselves in light of some religious principles or divine perspective? Perhaps theology is not fundamentally about understanding or explaining the self or the world. Rather, theology ought to be ordered toward change or transformation rather than understanding or explanation. Whether the change is to be wrought in the inner self or in societies, whether the goal is inner peace or liberation, theology is for the sake of transformation.

Similarly, it can be argued that theology ought to be practical. All theology should translate directly into practice. Here, the emphasis is not on knowledge for its own sake, but the knowledge that can be used. Or, what do I need to know to do certain tasks? Knowledge is the acquisition of skills. This task or skill oriented theology can re-shape how we learn theology. Theological education, especially for the ministry of the church, becomes accountable to how well it prepares persons to perform an array of ministerial tasks. The purpose of theology is to prepare people to perform tasks or to practice skills. Use becomes a cipher for knowledge. Theology gets us ready to act. Just as an identified concern in the church or in the world can shape the theology designed to address this concern, theology can be designed for its intended use. Theology can be constructed according to a plan of action. The grid of ministerial tasks becomes the grid of knowledge. This approach to theology places the emphasis on the learner or consumer. The consumer asks what do I need to know to do what I want to do? Theology exists in the background of human action and identity. Theology serves our actions.

This consideration of the relationship between theology and human action, framed by the question of the purpose of theology, is rooted in a fundamental theological orientation. The theological relationship between knowledge and action, however understood, reflects what one considers the basic movement or orientation of theology. The concept of movement offers a critical analysis of what is involved in the nature and task of theology. In the discussion above, I characterized an approach to theology and theological education whereby knowledge serves action, knowledge for the sake of performance. This is a movement from acquiring knowledge to application of that knowledge. The method of acquiring, and the scope of knowledge, is accountable to its application. This is the movement from knowing to doing. In the theological sphere, knowledge is gained in order to perform the basic actions of the Christian faith or of the church. Examples of such faithful action would be liberating the oppressed, growing local churches, proclaiming the Gospel, and counseling persons in crisis. Sometimes, the relationship between theological knowledge and application can be pressed further so that knowledge is gained with application. Adequate theological knowledge for application is garnered by theological reflection on application, knowing emerges from doing. Practical theology is not only a theology that can be practiced, practice yields theological understanding. Faithful action is the crucible from which an adequate theological knowledge or understanding of that action develops. One does not just know in order to act, one acts in order to know. Whether personal faithful action, or ecclesial practice, theological knowledge is generated by reflection on human action. This action may be motivated by profound theological concerns, but it remains human action that guides understanding. This is the theological turn to the acting subject rather than the existential subject, e.g., Rahner's anthropological starting point.

Contrasted with the theological movement from knowledge to application, and knowledge from application, is the movement of participation. Here, theology is a reflection on our participation in the divine reality or life. Through reflection arising from normative modes of participation, we attain reflective knowledge. That is, participation is not just the way to knowledge, it is the nature of theological knowledge. Theological knowledge is normatively participatory knowledge. Knowledge is qualified always by the reality in which the knower participates, and in a derivative sense, by the mode of participation. Participatory knowledge never exhausts itself. We do not know everything about what we know. Knowing is an act of offering; the self is subjected to an other or otherness. Hence, knowledge is subjective, but this subjectivity is not just a function of the self. Subjectivity is not comprised of collapsing knowledge into the categories of the self, but includes the discovery of the self in the participatory presence of an other.

Participatory knowledge can seem ambiguous when compared to knowledge produced by the mind, or knowledge that equips the self for action. The knower is not absolute as thinker or doer. Because participation is a movement to a reality inherently more expansive than the participant, and a particular act of participation, knowledge attained by participation is always partial, and perhaps, provisional. While the theological movement from knowledge to application is knowledge for the sake of action, the movement of participation to knowledge is action for the sake of knowing.

What is a normative participatory theological act? The applicative theological act privileges the primacy of the human agent, whether the proclaiming agent or the liberating agent. It is ordered toward a performance that accomplishes or achieves its aim. The human person remains that acting agent, the one who acts throughout the action toward a specified goal. The participatory theological act privileges the divine agent. It is not primarily a movement from God to the world; it is a movement from the world to God, so that God may act on it and within it. The applicative approach speaks of our God-authorized or God-directed action in the world. The participatory approach is our action from and with the world so that God may act on it. The basic theological move is to place the world before God and to ask God to act. In this way, the theological act is a passive action. Fundamentally, God's actions do not serve as examples for our faithful actions. Rather, our actions are a movement toward God's actions.

Fidelity is exercised toward the normative places and modes, the events, of God's actions. Instead of God acting so we can act, we act so God can act. Similar to the difference between applicative and participatory knowledge, there is a decisive contrast between applicative and participatory action. Participatory action does not have the definitiveness or clarity of applicative action. Since the goal of our action is not our own accomplishment, we are tempted to seek a pattern of faithful action that reflects directly on our efforts and indirectly on God's efforts. Applicative action can lead to theological reflection on human action at the expense of a theological reflection on God's actions. We can focus on what we can do, or what we should do, or how do we do it, rather than the concern that all our actions, and our theological reflections, are always in the passive voice. In the mode of participatory action and knowledge, theology must not pursue the ends of human accomplishment with its own criteria of appreciation, or human knowledge that constructs its own clarity. Accomplishment and clarity will not yield to transformation and doxology. Human action and knowledge exist as our participation within the superfluity of God's will and nature.

Within the participatory movement from action to knowledge, the normative theological act is constituted by prayer and worship. Theology is characterized by contemplation, adoration, memory, and invocation. These normative participatory theological acts do not exclude other acts, such as the applicative ones. Rather, as normative acts they shape the understanding and performance of other acts.

The preceding discussion of the theological relationship between knowledge and action, and the contrast between the theological movements of application and participation, began with the question of the purpose of theology. Differences regarding the purpose of theology can account for the plurality of theologies. How one identifies the purpose of theology can lead to an emphasis on a particular theological discipline, or on an intellectual or methodological partner for theology. For example, if theology is equipping us for faithful action, then we might stress personal or social ethics. Likewise, theology can be the preparatory work for preaching, because the purpose of theology is viewed as primarily proclamation. If theology is ordered toward participation in the divine life, then theology might focus on prayer, worship, and sacraments. Depending upon the basic purpose of theology, and its requisite emphases, theologians might employ other intellectual disciplines as partners in the theological task. Examples of other disciplines would be philosophical ethics, political and social thought, ritual studies, and all the subdisciplines of philosophy.

Variety within theology or plurality of theologies can be accounted for in terms of the intellectual climate in which theology is done. The question of intellectual climate has diachronic and synchronic scope. Intellectual climate has changed throughout history as well as there being different intellectual climates currently existing. Prior to the question of how and to what extent the intellectual climate shapes or informs theology, there is the basic question whether theology should engage this climate in any positive way. Historically, this is the abiding question of the relationship between theology and philosophy. Should there be a positive relationship between theology and philosophy? Should theology think about its subject in the prevailing way that others think? Should theology appropriate its own history in a way that would be recognizable by anyone who studies history? Should nontheological understandings of the mind, knowledge, truth, and reality inform, or even transform, theology? Or, should any intellectual discipline, with its methods and content, remain outside the proper theological sphere?

In the history of theology, apologetics has been the effort to give an account of the Christian faith in light of current philosophical understandings of self and of world. In the modern period, apologetics also includes a theological encounter with the natural sciences. Theologians have sought to explain the basics of the Christian faith in terms and concepts found in other intellectual disciplines with their accounts of truth and of reality, or of self and of the world. Customarily, apologetics establishes a common ground between theology and philosophy, or between faith and reason, in order to gain a hearing for the Christian faith outside of the church, or to defend the faith from challenges to it. This apologetic move from theology to philosophy is distinguished from the way in which theologians have incorporated philosophical concepts and methods for the purpose of clarifying or of expressing theological understandings. This is the difference between adapting philosophy to theology and adopting philosophical ideas for theology.

FAITH SEEKING UNDERSTANDING

The relationship between theology and philosophy, or between theology and any discipline for understanding the self and the world, takes a variety of directions. These directions can be appreciated within the characteristic movements theology makes toward its goal (whatever it is), and especially if the goal is understanding of God and/or self and world. (The question of whether one can understand God without some effort to understand self and/or world is laid aside for now.) One traditional way of expressing the theological movement of understanding is Anselm's definition of theology as faith seeking understanding. This movement of seeking can be characterized in three basic ways: within to within; within to without; and without to within.

Faith seeking understanding can be approached as a theological movement within the church: the faithful seek to understand the faith. Here, theology is the science of faith. Theology works directly and exclusively with and within the normative and authoritative sources of God's revelation. The object of understanding is God's special or historical revelation. Usually, Scripture is the primary, if not the only, source of theology. This approach to theology is not concerned with giving an account of reality outside the formal bounds of the community of the faithful or/and of the Scriptural narrative. Understanding the Word of God is the chief task of theology, a task meant to serve the church's proclamation of this same Word of God. Scripture is the norm that is normative for all else. Scripture is not understood or interpreted on the world's terms. Rather, the world is understood or interpreted on Scripture's terms. The apologetic task of establishing common ground between theology and philosophy is assiduously avoided. Employing any modes of understanding that are found outside the Christian faith and revelation would distort or dilute the Christian faith. Human reason is not granted its own sphere of operation that could shape theology in any positive way.

A second way to approach faith seeking understanding is characterized by the theological movement of within to without. On the basis of an understanding of the faith, theologians seek to understand what lies outside of faith. Faith provides the concepts and perceptions for understanding reality as a whole, even though some areas of reality have their proper disciplines for understanding. Faith is the point of departure for understanding realities that serve as the first concern of other intellectual disciplines, i.e., anthropology, philosophy, sociology, or the various branches of the natural sciences. Theologians will engage conversations already taking place outside of faith, but they will do so as theologians, as those who strive to say something meaningful about God no matter what the presenting subject is. The supposition is that theology can and should offer its own distinctive contribution to any discourse about truth, meaning, value, or understanding as well as challenge and inform other contributions. In this way, theologians reach for a comprehensive and coherent understanding of God, self, and world rooted in the Christian faith.

The third movement of seeking understanding is from without to within. Theologians adopt and/or adapt ways of understanding found in other disciplines for the purpose of understanding the Christian faith. The movement begins with an investigation of a method or mode of understanding reality or history or text, and then applying this method to a corresponding feature of the Christian faith. The supposition is that the Christian faith ought to be understood the way we understand anything. Theology does not comprise a different realm of understanding regarding the nature and methods of human knowing. Rather, Christian faith offers a different object that one strives to understand the way one would understand other objects of disciplined study. How we (recognizing that the "we" can be a conflicted question appealing to a variety of knowing subjects) understand language, culture, ritual, self, the physical and metaphysical world, would be employed in the task of understanding a corresponding area of theology. For example, methods arising from linguistic and textual studies would guide Scriptural studies. However, the adoption of modes of understanding from outside of theology for the purpose of understanding the Christian faith is not a neutral undertaking. The content studied is mediated by the way we study it. This movement of seeking can yield a faith shaped or reconstructed by the way we understand it. How we understand something shapes what we understand. Knowledge is a product of the knower, the knowing, and the known.

These three possible movements of seeking, occurring in the theological relationship between faith and understanding, provide another perspective on the plurality of approaches to the nature and method of theology. Determinative questions of ecclesial context, the self, authoritative sources, concerns, and intellectual framework can be arranged according to their relative importance or emphasis depending on which of the three movements is operative. For example, the movement within to within will stress the role of Scripture forming the faithful community, while the movement without to within will occupy itself with contemporary questions of epistemology in its reinterpretation of the Christian faith. The movement within to without might seek a common understanding of the self on which the Christian faith can be taught or conveyed.

All of these considerations of the plurality of theology, and whatever taxonomy we might choose to describe it, has not answered the question with which we began: What is theology, and its attending question, how should theology be done? I have surveyed briefly the scope of considerations that are brought to these questions. Any answer to them, or any constructive proposal, should be aware of these various approaches to the nature and method of theology. For theology is multidimensional, and however one speaks of the nature and method of theology, each of the dimensions should be addressed. At this point, I will begin to present what I consider the basics of any answer to the two presenting questions. More directly, I will seek to articulate the normative criteria for Christian theology, what I take to be the given suppositions for any Christian theological endeavor.

THEOLOGY IS ABOUT JESUS

Christian theology grants primary place to the person and work of Jesus Christ. This is the place of departure and accountability. However, it is not an isolated place. Theology is not just about Jesus Christ, because Jesus was not just about himself. Attending to Jesus is brought into the revelation of God, and into humanity, within this revelation. Attending to Jesus makes us aware of his message and ministry regarding the approach of the kingdom of God. Theology is not synonymous with Christology. The revelation of God as God in Jesus opens a vista of knowing and doing that reaches into every corner of reality. And yet, the implications of theology for the whole of reality should not lead to the plurality of a fragmented reality.

Christian theology is about Jesus Christ; it is about the historical person of Jesus revealed as the Christ. Being about Jesus Christ does not mean that theology must say something about Jesus at some point in the course of its work. This "about" is theology being rooted in Jesus Christ, who comprises the abiding reality of accountability. Rooted in Jesus Christ, theology works within and from the historical-existential-temporal exigencies of Jesus. Theology is done within and from the historical-existential-temporal exigencies of the theologian, and the place, person, and event that is the presence of Jesus has its own proper historical-existential-temporal exigencies. Here, we recognize that for theology to be about Jesus, theology engages not in an a-historical or a-temporal phenomenon, not a person without flesh. Flesh will not allow flight away for particularity and exigency. Flesh only exists as an historical-existential-temporal reality. The Word becoming flesh means that we do not have the Word without flesh. Likewise, flesh as a *theological* reality is Word-ed flesh.

The nature and method of theology lies within and from the nexus between Jesus and those who wish to understand him, know him, speak about him, and live with and in him. This nexus is never abstract or contrived; it must be recognized as the place of accountability and of generation. The nexus is the historical, existential, and temporal place where and how the historical-existential-temporal Jesus engages our historical-existential-temporal selves. Such engagement—the Word who became flesh and who, as such, is becoming present to us—does not allow us to speak of the Word without a flesh nor to speak of a flesh without the Word. That is, theology cannot speak of Jesus without history, existence, and time. Likewise, theology cannot speak of history, existence, and time, indeed, of all reality, without speaking of Jesus. Put in more formal theological terms, there is no Christological point-of-departure that is not also an anthropological one and vice versa. Theology is not about a-historical and a-temporal concepts nor about concepts confined by history and time. Theological understanding is always historical, existential, and temporal, and this understanding always involves more than history, existence, and time. Theology is accountable to, and generated from, a nexus with its proper historical, existential, and temporal exigencies, and yet, as nexus, it is an encounter between the exigencies of Jesus and the exigencies of the church. For this nexus to be the place and event of accountability and generation, it should exhibit a con-naturality of exigencies between Jesus and the church.

The nexus of theological accountability and generation has a tradition and a context. The nexus between Jesus and humanity that is the Christological reality is always a present offering to humanity as the possibility of salvation, a joining with Jesus that transforms humanity or the human self into the form of Christ. The nexus that is Jesus is present throughout the history of the church as the offer of the salvific nexus. The nexus is an event and reality in history; it has a history, and it can make history. The nexus between God and humanity in Jesus, and the engagement between Jesus and humanity, and the possibility for engagement, means that theology always operates across the continuum of past, present, and future. Theology has a history of accountability to Jesus and a tradition of generation. Tradition is a witness to accountability and generation.

Theology is about Jesus; and as such, theology is accountable to, and generated from, the reality of Jesus. This reality is present with a tradition (accountability) and with a vision (generation). The presence of Jesus is an invitation to dwell with him and in him. Those who respond to this invitation gather together, and this gathering provides the context for formation and fidelity. The nexus between Jesus and humanity forms a people bound to Jesus and bound to each other. To be rooted in Jesus is to be rooted as his faithful community. If theology is about Jesus, then theology is an ecclesial operation. Theology works through ecclesial accountability and ecclesial generation. Theology is an activity of the church and as the church, but theology is not *about* the church. The church is the mode and context of accountability and generation when theology is properly about Jesus. Theology is about Jesus in the way that the church is about Jesus. In this way, theology should serve the ecclesial life as a life accountable to what it means to be about Jesus, and as a life generated from being about Jesus. Likewise, the church provides parameters and directions for theology, if theology is to remain fixed on being about Jesus. Theology is accountable to, and generated from, the *theological* life of the church, the life that was, is, and will be, about Jesus.

Theology is done from the normative nexus between Jesus and the church: the place and event where and whereby Jesus is present as the nexus between God and humanity, and where and whereby humanity is invited to encounter Jesus for the renewal of life that comes from receiving the life of Jesus. Theology lives from this place and event of renewal—renewal, because the encounter is always new and repeated. This is where and whereby theology is renewed in being about Jesus. Theology is accountable to, and generated by and from, the place and event where and whereby Jesus, who is about everything, is present as the invitation for everything to be about him. Therefore, this particular place and event has universal and comprehensive scope. Theology is to work from this place and event and out toward the full scope and spectrum of humanity, creation, and cosmos. Theology lives from and by the place and event where and whereby Jesus lives as the invitation and the offering for the life of the world.

Theology will be concerned with the world, but not primarily as the world concerns itself. Theology approaches the world from the place and event of Jesus' invitation and offering. Theology will abide with being about Jesus within the ecclesial context as theology takes on the nature and concerns of the world for the sake of the renewal and the transformation of the life of this world when it becomes about Jesus. Regarding the three options of approach to Anselm's definition of theology outlined above, I am arguing for the movement of within to without. Faith seeks to deepen its understanding within the church and moves out toward understanding the world. Theology is about Jesus, and as such, theology is about all that is called to share his life. Theology will keep certain questions at the forefront: How is Jesus alive for the world; and, how can the world be alive in Jesus, live into Jesus?

Theology should take up questions of the self, culture, language, and philosophy, but it should do so from the event and context of accountability: the event of Jesus within the church and for the world. Furthermore, the question of the sources of theology should be approached in terms of the living presence of Jesus as invitation to transformation, as offering seeking mutuality. Sources of theology, and the more comprehensive question of revelation, ought to be considered as this living presence of Jesus, with the offer of the transformative nexus having historical-existential comprehensive scope.

The originating questions of this discussion concerned the nature and method of theology. I have begun to lay the groundwork for answering these questions. I have argued that the normative and accountable point of departure is the event of the offering and invitation of the living Jesus into the transformative nexus between God, humanity, and the world. Furthermore, I have argued that theology is about Jesus and is an ecclesial reality. In order to explore in more depth the questions of the nature and method of theology, a prior determinative question suggests itself: why theology?

THE ARRIVAL OF JESUS

In the above discussion, I broached the question of why theology when I addressed the question of the purpose of theology, and how one's notion of purpose shapes an understanding of the nature and method of theology. Asking why theology is a more fundamental question. I am considering not just why we do theology, or where will the exercise of theology take us; but, why theology at all. Of course, asking the why of anything carries an implicit conception of what you are asking about. To ask why theology includes some implicit notion of what it is already. However, by exploring the question of why theology at all, I hope to gain a greater appreciation of what I have begun to say regarding the nature and method of theology. The why question will provide a deeper sense of the direction initiated here for theology.

If theology is fundamentally about Jesus, and not only about Jesus, but about God, self, church, and world insofar as they are either revealed by, or transformed through him, then to ask why theology is to ask why Jesus. Hence, we should say that theology is not only about Jesus, but theology is contingent upon him. Theology is from, with, in, and toward Jesus. Likewise, we would say that Jesus is from, with, in, and toward God. Why theology is contingent upon why Jesus. Now, in addressing the question of why Jesus, I am not beginning to construct a formal Christology or soteriology. My purpose is to make some preliminary remarks, or assumptions, that facilitate and further the project of providing some fundamental direction for the nature and method of theology.

Jesus is God as a human, given within human history, so that humanity can live into God, and history can become transformed by, and fulfilled as, the Kingdom of God. Jesus is God's entrance, which is distinct from witness or agent only, into human life and history. This entrance of God provides humanity and creation with an entrance into God as a God-given and God-redeemed reality. Jesus is the arrival of God, and Jesus is the way that humanity, creation, and history arrives to and toward God. Jesus is God's arrival and the hope of human arrival. Certainly, the divine and human natures of the one person are included in this arrival. And yet, arrival is an event, an ongoing dynamic, a movement, and is all this as well. Jesus is a living presence that cannot be confined by, or limited to, all of our ways of defining and locating presence. Jesus is present to us as we are in the present. And, the presence of Jesus is the arrival of the future. Likewise, the presence of Jesus brings a presence that is not ours. Life with Jesus begins with his arrival as an arriving life. This means that the terms, the dimensions, the self-understandings of our life, and of our presence and present, must lie open to the arrival of Jesus. Flesh must always be willing to be Word-ed, to become the incarnation of God ordered toward being raised into God.

The incarnation of God is for the sake of a resurrected humanity. We do not understand Jesus by understanding the tomb or any other human, historical, or cultural place that somehow has Jesus in it. We do not locate the tomb and then locate Jesus. This is why fundamentally theology is not locating some fixed place where Jesus can be found. Theology does not start with where we are located culturally, historically, biologically, or intellectually. Theology starts where and when Jesus arrives, and theology ought to be the faithful exercise derived from his arriving. Theology is not about where we come from, nor the context of our human presence. Being about Jesus, theology is about the arrival of Jesus and our responsive arrival in him. Theology begins with this arrival and faithfully follows the path of our arrival to the Father, in the Son, and by the Spirit. Theology asks the question, Where and how does Jesus arrive? Likewise, theology asks, Where and how is Jesus taking us? This is why theology properly poses the questions of human understanding, culture, historical context, and intellectual climate as places and realities of Jesus' arrival. All that theologically constitutes our present and presence are Jesus' ways to us, and not primarily, our ways to Jesus. Theologically, we do not find our own way and then find Jesus. Jesus finds us, and bids us to follow him along the way to the Father.

Where and how does Jesus arrive in order to take us from where we are to where we might be? Before addressing this question directly; that is, prior to the development of the proper theological answer and its agenda for theology, the nature and scope of Jesus' arrival should be considered briefly. Jesus arrives as the risen one. Jesus arrives as one who has departed and then returns. He arrives as one who has departed the definitions of creation, of location, and of time. He has departed all forms of arrival that are transfers from one defined place and time to another. He no longer moves within the continuum of creation or nature, place, and time. And yet, he arrives, but his arrival is of a completely different order of arrival, the arrival of the departed. As the risen one, Jesus can arrive anywhere at anytime and in any way. The nature, method, and location of his arrival is an exercise of his freedom. Having departed spatial, natural, and temporal definitions, his arrival is free from these definitions. Jesus' arrival is one of freedom and as freedom. Any speaking of Jesus' arrival-the where and the how-cannot be an absolute claim. However, while we cannot make absolute or exclusive claims for Jesus' arrival, we can speak normatively. Jesus arrives in order for us to encounter him. As arrival, it is an event with natural, spatial, and temporal dimensions. Jesus arrives at a place, a time, and to someone or some people. The arrival of Jesus cannot be defined by the people, the place, or the time of arriving; however, his arrival includes all of these dimensions. His arrival is his advent: Jesus comes into so as to come toward. Those who are present there and then are invited to encounter the risen and arriving Jesus and to respond to this encounter. Jesus arrives in order to take. The arrival of the departed one is the invitation to arrive where one is not. The place and time of Jesus' arrival is also the departure of that place and time from its present definitiveness. People, places, and times become re-defined by the arrival of the one who has departed the definitions of all people, all places, and all times. Theology proper exists at and from this event of arrival and re-definition.

The nature and method of theology are derived from the event of Jesus' arrival in the church and for the life of the world. Theology ought to be about Jesus the way the church is about Jesus. Theology will live from and as the normative event of Jesus' arrival with the invitation to share his life. For this arrival is, above all, for the sake of others to enter into his life. Jesus arrives to offer his life to others. This offer is primary and paradigmatic. We can appreciate the arrival of the invitation to, and offer of, Jesus' life by contrasting it with the other possible primary and paradigmatic reasons for this arrival. Jesus could arrive in order to teach, judge, heal, fix, show, encourage, enlighten, direct, motivate, help, affirm, forgive, justify, and so on. All of these options are current in the church, in theology, and in popular piety of various sorts. They all can have a proper place in Christian faith, but their place is not primary and paradigmatic. All of these reasons for the arrival of Jesus can be entertained as dimensions of that arrival, as dynamics of Jesus' offer of his life.

When Jesus arrives he offers his life. Again, my purpose is not to construct a formal Christology but to put forth the basic notion of what I am proposing. Jesus arrives to offer his life of communion, and this arrival is the event from which theology is done and how it is done. The nature of Jesus' arrival becomes the nature of theology, and the economy of this arrival is the work of theology. Therefore, the Christian faith is about Jesus' life of communion.

Already, I have qualified my understanding of Jesus' life by saying it is "his life of communion." The life of Jesus is not a solitary personal project; it is not an individual life. His life reveals the life of other persons insofar as the life of others is related to his life. Such life is the revelation of a life that is more than its defining boundaries. His life reveals a life he shares with others. The life of Jesus has a history realized in a time and place through his freedom to act. The life of Jesus has an historical existence and is available as an historical existence. His life has a history and can make history. Jesus lived a life of communion with God. Jesus lived the life of God's communion. The history of Jesus' life comprises the history of God's life of communion. Jesus arrives in history with this history to offer his life of communion to others in the way that he shares this life and is this life. Jesus offers what he receives; he offers what he is. Because Jesus arrives with the offer of his life of communion, the life he shares and is, the event of this arrival will be one of communion. We receive the offer of communion as communion. The faithful response to Jesus' offer is to receive his life of communion, to be in communion with him, to share in his life of communion with others, both human and divine.

Participation in Jesus' life of communion cannot be contained, self-defined, or self-limited. Understanding this life will always be qualified by the insistence that it is a life received and not self-constructed. Yet, this received life is to be lived in a place and time, and through the freedom to act. Our understanding of Jesus' life of communion issues from our faithful response to its offer, our reflection upon our participation in this life. We inhabit what we seek to understand, and the economy of our understanding shares in, and reflects, the economy of the life we inhabit. The ways of Jesus' life of communion as offered upon his arrival are the ways that we receive and inhabit this life, and the ways we seek to understand Jesus' life and our lives within and toward it.

EUCHARISTIC SYSTEMATIC THEOLOGY

In light of the perspective on the nature of theology presented thus far, I will reconsider the definition of theology as faith seeking understanding. We inhabit what we seek to understand. The object of our understanding exists within the context of our understanding, and we do not take up a place outside of this context in order to understand. We do not approach the object of understanding from a self-protected distance. We do not strive for a presence that is objective in the sense that what we wish to understand is placed over against us. Faith, as the starting point of theology, is something we inhabit. Theological understanding takes place within the habits of faithful living. Likewise, faith itself is not an inert object awaiting our analytical investigation. Faith is the dynamic of life for those who seek to understand it.

Inhabiting what we seek to understand, we understand faith in the ways that faith works. The economy of understanding derives from the economy of the faith and of faithful living. For the moment,

I am speaking of both *fides quae creditur* (the content of faith) and *fides qua creditur* (the living of faith). In order to understand faith, we inhabit faith, and we work within, and work from, faith's inherent understandability. We do not construct a method of understanding from other places or forms of understandability and then apply it to faith. We do not move from understanding to faith. We learn the ways of understanding that issue from inhabiting faith, and we practice these ways in all our efforts at understanding. This does not mean necessarily that all other efforts of understanding, all other epistemological methodologies, will be alien to faithful ways of understanding. For now, I am not taking up the question of natural theology, but I am placing normative theological understanding within the inhabitation of faith. We make our intellectual home within faith, and when we venture into foreign lands, we do so as those formed by another place but willing to listen and to learn from what will always be a foreign country.

Theology is seeking the understanding of faith as faith lives from our response to the arrival of Jesus with his offer of his life of communion. The ways of faith are derived from the ways that Jesus arrives offering us his life of communion. The ways of this offer, and the ways we respond to it, are the ways we inhabit faith, and therefore, the ways of theological understanding. Again, this means that we must first attend to the ways of the offer and response, the event of communion, before we adopt them for theological understanding. We learn how to do theology from the theological life. The nature of theology reflects the nature of the event of Jesus' offer and of our faithful response. Faith seeking understanding originates in, and is formed by, the event of Jesus' arrival offering his life of communion. This is the normative theological event that norms all other theological events.

The Eucharist is the event of the arrival of Jesus offering his life of communion within the church, and the Eucharist is the event of our normative response to this offer. As such, the Eucharist is the theological event from which derives the proper nature and method of theology. Theology is a Eucharistic faith seeking a Eucharistic understanding. While not all theological questions and concerns are found directly within the Eucharist, all of these questions and concerns should be pursued Eucharistically. This means that we learn theology as we inhabit the Eucharist and practice its economy of fidelity. Theological understanding, both its nature and method, is learned within the Eucharist. While theology originates from within the Eucharist, it moves out from the Eucharist to the church and to the world, seeking a Eucharistic understanding of church and of world. That is, theological faithfulness to the Eucharistic economy is the movement from within to without as the interpreted definition of faith seeking understanding. Why? Because Jesus' arrival in the Eucharist is the foundation of the church's life and for the life of the world. The offer of Jesus' life of communion is made for the sake of the whole world, for the sake of all reality brought into communion with God, and consequently, with itself. However, the movement from within to without, from the Eucharist through the church toward the world, is not the ultimate salvific movement; it is a movement for the sake of another movement. The ultimate movement is the gathering of the church and of the world into the life of God, a movement to the Father, through the Son, and by the Holy Spirit. This a gathering movement of without to within, the gathering of the world through the transformative waters of baptism into the sanctuary of the Eucharist, the place and event of living in communion with God, with each other, and with creation. The basic saving movement is arrival within the Eucharist, our encounter with the arriving Jesus, and our sharing in the future Kingdom of Heaven. Jesus' arrival within the Eucharist, and our arrival within the Eucharist, is theology's Alpha and Omega, its beginning and its end.

Theology is a Eucharistic faith seeking a Eucharistic understanding for the sake of a Eucharistic life. It is within the Eucharist that theology discovers its sources and the way to engage them, and the way they relate to each other. This Eucharistic thesis for theology, and for its systematic development and exposition, will be rooted first in the history of Jesus and then related to basic theological questions and categories.

I have argued that theology is our response to the arrival of Jesus, and that theology is shaped by the economy of the event of this arrival, i.e., the Eucharist. Speaking of arrival and of event is to speak historically. Theology is not thought above history, but thought within and from history, within and from a series of events, actions, and sustained practices. God is the object and subject of theology who brings God's own objectivity and subjectivity to bear on our sense of what is known (object) and who knows (subject). God does not say think about me while I think about you. Rather, the Word was made flesh and dwelled among us. God in the person of Jesus entered the course of human history to the point of being vulnerable to this history. God arrived in history and was available to what can happen to us through human agency. In the resurrection, God arrives in the person of Jesus with the dawning of a new history, what can happen to us through divine agency. Theology is located at the fulcrum event whereby human history (human agency) is transformed into divine history (divine agency). We locate this fulcrum event in the history of Jesus within the transition from human to divine agency.

Jesus' institution of the Eucharist at the Last Supper was the provision for his historical acting presence for the future that is meant to be shaped by him. He instituted, at the moment when his human history was about to conclude, the way in which his future divine history would be available to his disciples. In this Eucharistic way, Jesus is to arrive within human history, an event involving human agency, with his offer to receive, to participate in, the divine history of resurrection. Facing death, Jesus provides his disciples with the way to share his life. As his departure draws near, Jesus institutes his arrival. While he still maintains his agency, he commands his disciples to do something in his memory. For later that night he will be handed over to other agents. The institution of the Eucharist is his last act before undergoing the actions of other agents, human and divine, in his death and resurrection. Jesus provides the event whereby his risen arrival will take place, the principal event to encounter him. As such, the Eucharist is the primary and paradigmatic event for theological work and understanding. The Eucharist is the accountable structure for all theological endeavors because it the normative event of Jesus' arrival in the church for the life of the world. I have argued that theology is about Jesus the way the church is about Jesus. I have located the centrality of the Eucharist for theology in the history of Jesus. The normative way to be about Jesus is the Eucharist. I say normative, because I do not claim that Jesus is present only within the Eucharist, or one cannot be about Jesus in other ways. Rather, the Eucharist is the fullness of all ways to be about Jesus, and it is the paradigm for how these other ways are really about Jesus, and how these ways should be related to each other. For example, Scripture is about Jesus, and confessing sin and seeking forgiveness is about Jesus. My Eucharistic thesis for theology directs that the way of Scripture, and the way of forgiveness of sins, find their paradigmatic place within the Eucharist, where we also consider how these two ways are related to each other. Theology is about Jesus the way the church is about Jesus and this "about" is the Eucharist. Having located the Eucharistic thesis within Christology, I will locate it within ecclesiology.

The origins of the church reside within the origins of the celebration of the Eucharist. The gathering of Christians as the church was a gathering for the Eucharist. The centrality of the experience and understanding of the life of the church was rooted in, and shaped by, the Eucharist when Christians gathered for the arrival of the risen Jesus in proclaimed word and within a blessed and shared meal. The church is first and foremost a Eucharistic reality. Thus, the formative theological life of the church is provided by the paradigmatic ecclesial event of the Eucharist. Theology operates from the Eucharist and within the church, and not within the church while gazing upon the Eucharist as an object of study, perhaps one among many such objects. Theology inhabits the church by abiding within the dynamics of the Eucharistic event. The economy of theology is derived from the economy of the Eucharist, which the church represents and shares. The continuum of this economy is Eucharist, church, and theology. However, these relationships are not uncritical ones nor mutually accountable to each other. Theology will be diligent in its exercise of the stewardship of the Eucharistic economy as enacted in the celebration of the Eucharist and in the comprehensive life of the church. Likewise, a Eucharistic church will call theology to account for not serving its life and its mission.

From within the Eucharist, we learn the nature and method of theology. Likewise, from within the Eucharist we learn what are the subjects and concepts with which theology works. We do not take theological categories conceived outside the Eucharist and fill them with some Eucharistic content. I am not talking about a Eucharistic version of a method of correlation whereby we give Eucharistic answers to non-Eucharistic questions. Rather, Eucharistic questions transform all theological questions. From within the Eucharist, we learn why and how theology can become and be developed as systematic theology. We make the connections among the basic subjects and concepts of theology as they are connected within the Eucharist. That is, we learn what "systematic" means within the Eucharistic economy.

All that I have been discussing and proposing can be summarized in the following Eucharistic thesis for theology: The Eucharist is the event of the arrival of Jesus within the church offering his life of communion, and the Eucharist is the event of our normative response to this offer. As such, the Eucharist is *the* theological event. The nature and method of theology is derived from the Eucharist. Theology is called to be ultimately and accountably Eucharistic. The Eucharist is the theological norm that should norm all theological endeavors.

This thesis does not presume that all possible theological questions and issues will arise directly from within the Eucharist. Instead, I argue that all theological concerns, of whatever origin or type, should be pursued Eucharistically: a Eucharistic faith seeking a Eucharistic understanding, the constructive movement from within to without. Therefore, what I am proposing is a Eucharistic systematic theology.

Eucharistic systematic theology recognizes the sources of theology as they appear within the Eucharistic economy, and it makes the connections between these sources as they are related within this economy. The way in which theology understands and pursues the systematic exposition of the customary topics of theology will be rooted in, and always shaped by, the Eucharistic nature of system. That is, we learn the nature and method of a system from the Eucharist. This does not mean that we impose a system on the Eucharist. Rather, the Eucharist imposes a system on theology: an arrangement and basic understanding of all theological subjects. Treatments of the Trinity, Christology, ecclesiology, eschatology, anthropology, and so on, will retain their Eucharistic origins and shape. These treatments will not be contained by the Eucharist proper, but they will be accountable to the Eucharistic economy and its derivative theological nature and method.

Eucharistic systematic theology should reflect the main task of theology Eucharistically conceived. The main task of theology is not to solve the intellectual problems of the day or to secure a place for theology within the modern or postmodern academy. Nor is the main task of theology to "construct" the Christian faith from a privileged intellectual, cultural, linguistic, or historical standpoint. All of these concerns will be present, but they will not provide the normative origin, sources, shape, and purpose of theology. The normative theological task is to abide within the Eucharist, to contemplate and enact its ways, and from within this accountable life and understanding, to learn Scripture, to learn tradition, to learn reason, to learn holiness, to learn mission, and to learn church. Theology is about the church the way the church is about Jesus. In the Eucharist, Jesus arrives to offer his life of communion for the life of the world. We go there to receive this gift and to live faithfully and responsively from it. Eucharistic systematic theology engages the full scope of theological concerns in order to reveal, shape, and illuminate them as dimensions of the Eucharistic reality, the invitation to share God's life of communion and to live this communion on earth as it is in heaven.

NOTES

1. TRADITION

1 Unless it appears within a quotation from another source, all citations from Scripture are from the *New Revised Standard Version*, New York: The National Council of Churches.
2 All quotations and references to original Eucharistic texts are taken from R.C.D. Jasper and G.J. Cuming, editors. *Prayers of the Eucharist: Early and Reformed*, 3rd ed. New York: Pueblo Publishing Company, 1987. Hereafter, *PEER*.

2. PRESENCE

1 For a lucid presentation of the various biblical and philosophical developments in the theology of Eucharistic presence, see William R. Crockett, *Eucharist: Symbol of Transformation*. New York: Pueblo Publishing Company, 1989, especially chapters 2 and 3. The book as a whole gives a good review of the salient periods in the history and theology of the Eucharist.
2 A standard study of the patristic background and of the main lines of development in the Reformation is Yngve Brilioth, *Eucharistic Faith and Practice Evangelical and Catholic*, trans. by A.G. Hebert. London: S.P.C.K., 1956.
3 Quoted from Crockett, p. 110.
4 *PEER*, p. 93.
5 *PEER*, p. 133.

3. SACRIFICE

1 *PEER*, p.162.
2 *Luther's Works*, American Edition, Volume 35, p. 88. Hereafter *LW*.
3 *LW* 35, p. 99.
4 All references to, and quotations of, the debates and submissions of the theologians at the first session of the Council of Trent are taken from the collection: *Concilium Tridentinum: Diariorum, Actorum, Epistularum, Tractatum Nova Collectio*. edited by the Societas Goerresiana. Freiburg im Breisgau: Herder and Co., 1901. This work will be referred to as *CT* with

volume and page number, and all quotations from the Latin are my translations.

5 *CT* VI/I 336.
6 *CT* VI/II 571.
7 *CT* VI/II 458.
8 *CT* VI/II 476.
9 *CT* VI/II 567–568.
10 *CT* VI/I 334.
11 *CT* VI/I 337.
12 *CT* VI/I 367.
13 *CT* VI/I 377.
14 *PEER*, 165.
15 *PEER*, 92.

4. CHURCH

1 *Corpus Mysticum: The Eucharist and the Church in the Middle Ages.* Translated by Gemma Simmonds. London, SCM Press, 2006: 88.
2 *Corpus Mysticum*, 260.
3 This account is taken with slight alterations from Massey Shepherd, *The Worship of the Church*, New York: The Seabury Press, 1952: 3–4.
4 Homily on John 6:41–59 in *Nicene and Post-Nicene Fathers*, edited by Philip Schaff. Peabody, MA: Hendrickson Publishers, fourth printing, 2004: Volume 7: 172.
5 Sermon 272, as quoted in J.-M.-R. Tillard, *Flesh of the Church, Flesh of Christ*, translated by Madeleine Beaumont. Collegeville, MN: The Liturgical Press, 2001: 42. Tillard provides many important quotations from Augustine with commentary on the relationship between the Eucharistic and ecclesial Body of Christ. The entire book is recommended for further reflection on the concept of Eucharistic ecclesiology.
6 In a similar fashion, the following chapter on the Eucharistic life follows these set of actions to reflect on the nature of this life. This next chapter considers the actions in more scope and depth.
7 For the following discussion of the Eucharist and the catholicity of the church, I am indebted to the work of John Zizioulas, especially the chapter "Eucharist and Catholicity," in *Being and Communion*. Crestwood, NY: St. Vladimir's Seminary Press, 1985.
8 *Smyrnaeans* 8, quoted in Paul McPartlan, *Sacrament of Salvation: An Introduction to Eucharistic Ecclesiology*. London: T&T Clark, 1995: 64. This book provides a valuable review of the development and implications of a Eucharistic ecclesiology.

6. THEOLOGY

1 As quoted from Alexander Schmemann, *The Eucharist: Sacrament of the Kingdom*, translated by Paul Kachur. Crestwood, NY: St. Vladimir's

Seminary Press, 1988: 13. For the argument that follows, I consider Schmemann's work to be a guiding companion on the way to a full Eucharistic systematic theology. See also his essay, "Theology and Eucharist," in *Liturgy and Tradition: Theological Reflections of Alexander Schmemann*, edited by Thomas Fisch. Crestwood, NY: St. Vladimir's Seminary Press, 1990.

SELECT BIBLIOGRAPHY

The following works represent three categories of selection. The first category consists of works that appear in the endnotes. Secondly, there are books that offer the reader a solid introduction to the basic topics of the Eucharist indicated by the chapter titles. The third category is comprised of a few works whose content reflects the perspective presented in this book.

Bradshaw, Paul F. *Eucharistic Origins*. New York: Oxford University Press, 2004.

Cabie, Robert. *The Eucharist. The Church at Prayer*, Volume II. Edited by A. G. Mortimort. New Edition. Translated by Matthew J. O'Connell. Collegeville, MN: The Liturgical Press, 1986.

Crockett, William R. *Eucharist: Symbol of Transformation*. New York: Pueblo Publishing Company, 1989.

Dufour, Xavier Leon. *Sharing the Eucharistic Bread: The Witness of the New Testament*. Translated by Matthew J. O'Connell. New York: Paulist Press, 1987.

Irwin, Kevin W. *Models of the Eucharist*. New York: Paulist Press, 2005.

Jasper, R.C.D. and G.J. Cuming, editors. *Prayers of the Eucharist: Early and Reformed*. Third Edition. New York: Pueblo Publishing Company, 1987.

Koening, John. *The Feast of the World's Redemption: Eucharistic Origins and Christian Mission*. Harrisburg, PA: Trinity Press International, 2000.

de Lubac, Henri. *Corpus Mysticum: The Eucharist and the Church in the Middle Ages*. Translated by Gemma Simmonds with Richard Price and Christopher Stephens. London: SCM Press, 2006.

Mazza, Enrico. *The Celebration of the Eucharist: The Origin of the Rite and the Development of Its Interpretation*. Translated by Matthew J. O'Connell. Collegeville, MN: The Liturgical Press, 1999.

McPartlan, Paul. *Sacrament of Salvation: An Introduction to Eucharistic Ecclesiology*. London: T&T Clark Ltd., 1995.

Meyer, Ben F., editor. *One Loaf, One Cup: Ecumenical Studies of 1 Cor 11 and Other Eucharistic Texts*. Macon, GA: Mercer University Press, 1993.

Mitchell, Nathan. *Real Presence: The Work of Eucharist*. Chicago, IL: Liturgy Training Publications, 2001.

Power, David N. *The Sacrifice We Offer: The Tridentine Dogma and Its Reinterpretation*. New York: Crossroad, 1987.

Power, David N. *The Eucharistic Mystery: Revitalizing the Tradition.* New York: Crossroad, 1992.

Powers, Joseph M. *Eucharistic Theology.* New York: The Seabury Press, 1967.

Schmemann, Alexander. *For the Life of the World.* Second edition. Crestwood, NY: St. Vladimir's Seminary Press, 1973.

——. *The Eucharist: Sacrament of the Kingdom.* Translated by Paul Kachur. Crestwood, NY: St. Vladimir's Seminary Press, 1988.

——. *Liturgy and Tradition.* Edited by Thomas Fisch. Crestwood, NY: St. Vladimir's Seminary Press, 1990.

Stevenson, Kenneth W. *Eucharist and Offering.* New York: Pueblo Publishing Company, 1986.

Stuhlman, Byron D. *A Good and Joyful Thing: The Evolution of the Eucharistic Prayer.* New York: Church Publishing Incorporated, 2000.

Tillard, J.-M.-R. *Flesh of the Church, Flesh of Christ: At the Source of the Ecclesiology of Communion.* Translated by Madeleine Beaumont. Collegeville, MN: The Liturgical Press, 2001.

Wells, Samuel. *God's Companions: Reimaging Christian Ethics.* Oxford: Blackwell Publishing, 2006.

Williams, Rowan. *Eucharistic Sacrifice—The Roots of a Metaphor.* Bramcote, Notts.: Grove Books, 1982.

Wybrew, Hugh. *The Orthodox Liturgy: The Development of the Eucharistic Liturgy in the Byzantine Rite.* Crestwood, NY: St. Vladimir's Seminary Press, 1990.

Zizioulas, John. *Being As Communion: Studies in Personhood and the Church.* Crestwood, NY: St. Vladimir's Seminary Press, 1985.

INDEX